NOTE INVESTING FUNDAMENTALS

Your Guide to Launching a *Successful* Note Business!

Martin Saenz, MBA, MS

Find these #1 best-selling books by Martin Saenz at
https://amazon.com/ in paperback, e-book, and audiobook.

Real Estate Note Investing Mentorship

Note Investing Made Easier
How to Buy and Profit from Distressed Mortgages

Secrets to Winning Government Contracts
How Any Small Business Owner Can Become
a Profitable Prime Federal Contractor in Twelve Months or Less

Note Investing Fundamentals
Your Guide to Launching a Successful Note Business

Cashflow Dojo
Build Your Home on Multiple Streams of Income

Contents

◆ ◆ ◆

Dedication

◆ ◆ ◆

This book is dedicated to Justin.
May you rest in peace.

Disclaimer

◆ ◆ ◆

This book is meant for purely informational purposes only. Due diligence is required before making any investment decisions. You should not construe this book or any portion therein as legal, tax, investment, or financial advice, or any other type of advice.

Nothing contained in this book constitutes a solicitation, recommendation, endorsement, or offer by NIME Publishing House, Martin Saenz, or any third-party service provider to buy or sell any securities or other financial instruments in this or in any other jurisdiction in which such solicitation or offer would be unlawful under the securities laws of such jurisdiction.

The content in this book is general in nature and does not address the circumstances of any particular individual or business entity. Nothing in this book constitutes professional or financial advice; nor does any information in this book constitute a comprehensive or complete statement of the matters discussed or the laws relating thereto. NIME Publishing and Martin Saenz are not fiduciaries by virtue of any person's use of or access to this book or any portion therein.

About the Author

◆ ◆ ◆

Martin Saenz, BA, MS, MBA, is a professional public speaker, thought leader, investor, best-selling author, and fund operator. Approachable, knowledgeable, and determined, he is a self-made entrepreneur and successful real estate investor driven to grow asset value, income, and knowledge for his company, investors, and partners. He currently runs a twenty-five-person operation in Sarasota, Florida, with his partner, Shawn Muneio, and manages around $75 million in mortgage notes, commercial real estate, and energy assets. Martin and his wife, Ruth, founded a successful government contracting startup, which they later sold in 2013 to focus on their mortgage notes and real estate portfolio.

An accomplished business owner, Martin Saenz holds a BA in philosophy from UT-San Antonio, an MBA from Drexel University, and an MS in project management from George Washington University. A mentor and industry thought leader, he regularly speaks at note and real estate investing conferences around the country, where he shares his proven real estate note-investing strategies.

Martin has written five Amazon best-selling books that teach readers how to develop and grow a real estate mortgage note-investing business, whether they're new to the industry or seasoned professionals.

Introduction

◆ ◆ ◆

Sometimes, when you're dreaming, you don't always work out the fine details—but you still believe. As a kid polishing and selling shiny rocks to all my neighbors, I envisioned myself making a ton of money and being my own boss. Although my polished-rock business never really took off—five-year-olds make notoriously subpar CEOs—I found my calling in note investing, and it has afforded me the lifestyle that entrepreneurial kid dreamed about. Sometimes our wildest wishes provide a fleeting glimpse of who we were always destined to be.

What, then, is your dream? Why are you reading this book?

This book is about leading you to financial freedom—whatever that means to you. Maybe it's the ability to spend more time with your family and less time with a boss who you feel doesn't have your best interests at heart. Or perhaps you've hit a crossroads in your life where you realize you have fallen behind on your financial goals and time is running short. Whatever the case, now is the best time to make a change. When we are young, we have the energy to put in the maximum level of effort. As we get older, however, our energy decreases, and life's circumstances take over. Make the most of your time now to secure your finances for the future. Note investing can grow your monthly passive income to do just that. This book will teach you how to make that happen.

I thought about that pebble-selling little boy as I was flying over Detroit on my way to speak at the Information Management Network Dana Point Conference. My speech, "Finding Distressed Product," focused on helping those just entering the note-investing field develop this fundamental skill. Oh, how far I'd come. I may have once been naïve about the world of business, yet there I was, about to provide an in-depth look at how to ensure others' note businesses succeeded.

This book is for entrepreneurs who have at least a basic understanding of note investing. You have spent energy learning or mastering the technique, and now it's time to work on the business side of things so you can scale your business accordingly. This will be easier for some than others. If you have been an employee your entire life, then learning a new technique likely comes naturally—your paycheck has depended on it. If you have owned a business, you understand that running the business can be as taxing as offering your product or service. Both perspectives are valuable.

In this book, I introduce the three Cs of forming a successful note-investing business—the creation phase, the control phase, and the cash flow phase—all while using a process that puts your core strengths and values first. I'll touch on who and what you need to be in the note marketplace and help you avoid the pitfall most investors make: believing "cash is king." In this book, I suggest that "cash" and "cash flow" are the results of doing all the right steps in the right order correctly over time. The real king is "deal flow." Those who create and foster the proper deal flow will dominate the note investment marketplace—or any space for that matter. Deal flow is king!

Part 1: The Creation Phase

CHAPTER 1

◆ ◆ ◆

Building a Financial Foundation for Your Note Business

I started my entrepreneurial journey in 2004 after being fired from a corporate job. Getting fired when I did, in many ways, was an opportunity. At that time, I managed a call center with about 120 employees, and it was tantamount to hell on earth. I had to address numerous emails each day and be on conference calls with people I couldn't stand. There were multiple bosses. It was a nightmare, but I endured it like everyone else in corporate America. It's tough to love your job when a company is trying to extract as much value as they can from you while paying you just enough to keep you from leaving.

After some serious self-reflection, however, I knew I couldn't thrive in corporate America. I was spending all my time and energy at work, gaining no value except a paycheck. It was transactional— a simple exchange. Working for someone who cares very little about you is almost always a lose-lose situation.

I wanted to spend time with the people I cared about most in life. Instead, I was spending all my time with strangers who cared little about me, and I was coming home tired and frustrated. I was giving the best hours in my day to someone who cared nothing about me, and if you're reading this book, you probably already understand what I mean. When you get home, there's nothing left in the tank to spend time with the people you care about. Getting paid for the value I bring to the marketplace was what I was missing, and I could only achieve that through business ownership.

Getting fired gave me the courage to take that leap. But even though I knew that step was right for me, it felt as though everyone was against me. And fair enough. Creating a business is hard. It can be lonesome work, but compared to the loneliness that comes from competitive corporatism, how bad could it be? When I finally realized that other people were getting rich off *my* labor, I knew I had to do something about it.

"How much worse can self-employment be?" I asked my wife one day. Ruth was tired of the corporate game as much as I was.

"It can't be," she said.

Ruth has always been by my side no matter what. She is a strong, intelligent woman, and we started our business in search of financial freedom. At first, we were hoping freedom would come from owning real estate, so we began landlording and buying commercial and residential properties. What we found, though, wasn't truly financial freedom.

Then we found real estate note investing in 2013 and discovered something better than financial freedom: freedom of time. Note investing takes a lot of different forms, and explaining the different models could be a book in and of itself. For the purposes of my journey, I found you can buy nonperforming mortgage notes at a discount and work with the homeowner to create a payment plan that will keep them in their home. While making a handsome profit, of course. I laid out this win-win model in *Note Investing Made Easier*.

If you're striving to take back time for yourself and your family, resuscitate your finances, start living on *your* terms, or take back your life and break free of the corporate paradigm that's keeping you from seeing your true potential, then note investing might be for you.

Start by picturing what your financially free life might look like. When we get into the road-mapping stage later, we will revisit this vision of the future. It will only come to fruition if you keep it as your heading and if you're willing to put in the work to achieve it. From there, this book will smooth out the learning curve for new note investors and strengthen the fundamentals of the seasoned ones so you can reach your vision of financial freedom.

Getting Your Financial House in Order

Whether you are new to note investing or have been at it for some time, you need to assemble and maintain a living financial statement. This document is a personal and business financial statement that connects your current financial situation with your goals. You will want to maintain it on a weekly basis and meet with an accountability partner who will help keep you on track with your goals. Since you are in the lending business, you need to know where you stand financially, the same as with any other financial business. Well, at least the successful ones.

For a living financial statement template, visit https://martinsaenz.com/.

OUR WHY: What is driving you to make this happen?

INCOME STATEMENT

INCOME				EXPENSES			
Description	Cash Flow	Description	Cash Flow	Description	Cash Flow	Description	Cash Flow
Active Income:				**Living Expenses:**		**Business Expenses:**	
Salary Job 1	$7,083			Food	$2,400	Real Estate Mtg #1	$750
Salary Job 2	$5,416			Utilities	$400	Real Estate Mtg #2	$2,800
				Credit Card	$350	Real Estate Mtg #3	$2,400
				Entertainment	$1,000	Vehicle Payment	$500
Passive Income:							
Income Funds		Misc.					
Income Fund #1	$8,333	Book Royalty	$500	Total Active Income:	$12,499	Total Living Expenses:	$4,150
Income Fund #2	$3,333	Private Equity Investment	$900			Total Expenses Goal:	$10,000
Income Fund #3	$1,500	Bitcoin Mining	$600	Total Passive Income:	$26,616	% to LI Goal:	241%
		Oil & Gas Operator Distributions	$1,000	Passive Income Goal:	$100,000	Amount to LI Goal:	-$5,850
Promissory Notes				% to PI Goal:	27%		
Real Estate Note #1	$200			Amount to PI Goal:	$73,384		
Real Estate Note #2	$500						
Real Estate Note #3	$50					Total Income:	$39,115
Bank CD #1	$200					Total Expenses:	$10,600
						Monthly Cash Flow:	$28,515
Real Estate							
Real Estate Property #1	$1,800						
Real Estate Property #2	$4,500						
Real Estate Property #3	$3,200						

Income and Expenses Section

In the income statement section, income is broken down between active income and passive income. As you get older, you need more monthly passive income to offset the active income, or at least complement it. You want to develop passive income goals and measure your performance against those goals on a weekly basis when you review your statement. I recommend laying out all the passive income streams under categories you define yourself.

In the expenses column, separate your living expenses from your business expenses. Living expenses are any expenses you need to live day-to-day. Business expenses are any expenses you incur procuring and maintaining assets that produce monthly passive income. With your living expenses separated out, you can work on budgeting your lifestyle expenses if that is the direction you seek.

The goal of filling out this first page is to understand clearly where you stand financially and how close you are to achieving your monthly passive income goals. This is at the heart of note investing.

BALANCE SHEET							
ASSETS					**LIABILITIES**		
Description	Amount	Description	Amount			Description	Amount
Banking:		Real Estate:		Income Fund Actual:	$1,700,000	Real Estate Mortgages:	
Bank #1	$125,000	Real Estate Property #1	$150,000	Income Fund Goal:	$8,000,000	Real Estate Property #1	$75,000
Bank #2	$45,000	Real Estate Property #2	$450,000	% to Goal:	21%	Real Estate Property #2	$250,000
Bank #3	$20,000	Real Estate Property #3	$325,000			Real Estate Property #3	$185,000
				Promissory Notes Actual:	$175,000		
		Misc.:		Promissory Notes Actual:	$3,000,000	Long Term Debt:	
		Book Royalty	$5,000	% to Goal:	6%	Student Loan	$35,400
Income Funds:		Private Equity Investment	$75,000	Retirement Actual:	$770,000	Vehicle Loan	$46,500
Income Fund #1	$1,000,000	Bitcoin Mining	$12,000	Retirement Goal:	$2,000,000		
Income Fund #2	$500,000	Oil & Gas Operator Distributions	$100,000	% to Goal:	39%	Short Term Debt:	
Income Fund #3	$200,000					Credit Card #1	$4,500
		Store of Value:		Real Estate Actual:	$925,000	Credit Card #2	$8,900
Promissory Notes:		Gold Coins	$8,000	Real Estate Goal:	$4,000,000		
Real Estate Note #1	$25,000	Silver Coins	$1,800	% to Goal:	23%		
Real Estate Note #2	$85,000	Bitcoin	$54,000				
Real Estate Note #3	$15,000			Bitcoin Actual:	2		
Bank CD #1	$50,000			Bitcoin Goal:	50		
				% to Goal:	4%		
Retirement Accounts:				Precious Metals Actual:	$9,800		
401k Program - Name #1	$350,000			Precious Metals Goal:	$1,000,000		
401k Program - Name #2	$200,000			% to Goal:	1%		
SDIRA - Name #1	$180,000						
SDIRA - Name #2	$40,000			Oil & Gas Actual:	$100,000	Total Assets:	54,015,800
				Oil & Gas Goal:	$2,000,000	Total Liabilities:	$605,300
				% to Goal:	5%	Networth:	$3,410,500

Assets and Liabilities Section

From here, break out your assets in terms of liquidity, passive income production, and store of value. The goal here is to make you aware of all your income-producing assets and organize them in a way that allows you to have better weekly discussions with your accountability partner. As with the income statement, you should set goals for asset generation. As a side strategy, I only acquire store-of-value assets with passive income. This helps remove emotion from investing.

In the liabilities section, my objective is to only take on liabilities that help me acquire cash-flowing assets. Hence, all debt would be good debt. The important thing to note here is how all the different sections work together. You will source assets that produce monthly passive income, and in some cases, you will take on liabilities that create business expenses.

Every morning when I get up, I have some coffee, and I go sit on the couch and take about five to seven minutes to meditate on being grateful for my life. Even if I'm having a bad week or a bad month, I think of all the reasons I have to be thankful—having friends, a house in Florida, a great income, even my dog, that sort of thing. Too many people live for today.

I call it visualization. I visualize where I'm going to be in five years. It took a while to see, but I literally sit on my couch for a few minutes, and I can see myself exactly where I'm going to be in five years. I can see the actual flip-flops I'm wearing, the boat I'm getting out of, riding my bike, and the ocean in the background. I see myself walking to the second floor of the house, and there are twenty windows, and I can look out across the water. I started this last year.

What I thought would be a five-year plan started moving even faster. I've already bought a house in the Keys. I think because of the visualization process—I might have gotten there otherwise—but it would have still been seven or eight years away.

It's so deep in my subconscious that I almost feel like it's a reality already.

That is my hope for your readers, Martin. It starts with belief, and you can visualize whatever you want to visualize. We took the word *fear* completely out of our vocabulary. And it's as you said, "It's free. Everyone can do it." That's certainly true too. It's not going to be easy, though. You have to practice at it for a while, but you can get there. —Steve Lloyd

We get stuck in the corporate world. We are barely making ends meet—if at all—and while we may be dreaming of a better way out, it feels practically impossible to make it happen.

"What is it in you that you're seeking to find?"

That's a fair question to ask people. I do so often. More than anything else, I hear financial freedom. People are looking for financial freedom, and I certainly understand that. I venture to say that most people who say financial freedom, when you drill a little deeper, are actually looking for freedom of time.

That's true freedom—the freedom not to be bound to corporate servitude in exchange for a paycheck; we sell our time. We feel trapped when we do this. In my case, I also sold my time, but I had very little to show for it. Perhaps that's your case as well, but you'll really want to dig deep and ask yourself what brought you to note investing versus other opportunities you had.

I also hear that people are looking for easy work schedules and quick results. They are looking to compensate for decades of poor decisions with their time and their finances. This is not a get-rich-quick game. It's a get-wealthy-slow game if you do all the necessary steps.

Successful note investors create market plans and business strategies, and they work the hell out of them on an ongoing basis. Most of them are focused on results. What you yield comes from what you seek. It's all the steps that you have to take on an ongoing basis to yield the particular results you're after.

If a certain bank account number appeals to you, or you want more time with your family—all of those things are end results or goals you should incorporate into your living financial statement. It's what it takes to get you to that point that is the key to unlocking those results.

I've been educating note investors for years, and I've learned so much about myself in that time. I learned what it takes to set up a successful business; I picked up some great techniques from my peers. I studied hard. I developed transformational results, and I did so consistently.

What I found was that many programs, whether they're in real estate or note investing specifically, lead you down a pathway where you are a perpetual student. They keep you in that student mindset indefinitely. What I want to do is drastically different. I want to mentor others with the express goal of transforming students into equal partners and colleagues. That means this book is as much about mindset as it is about the technical fundamentals of note investing. With the right mindset, you can build a successful note business model around your strengths and compensate for the weaknesses. As such, I take the best techniques and practices that I've learned and document them for you in this clear and easy-to-follow format. I cover the areas of self-reflection, setting up your branding, and due diligence in more detail in *Note Investing Made Easier* and *Real Estate Note Investing Mentorship*. Both of those books explain the mechanics of note investing, and this book completes the equation by covering the fundamentals of setting your business up.

In the following chapter, we will review my interview with Jason Osser, specifically as it relates to those best techniques and practices. He is a trusted friend and strategic partner.

CHAPTER 2

◆ ◆ ◆

Enhance Your Financial Foundation with the 3 Cs of Business

3 C's of Business

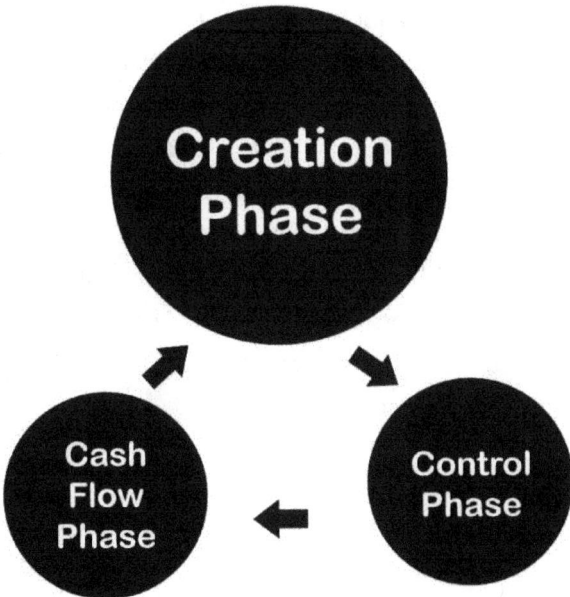

Since I put the 3 Cs of Business into practice several years ago, they've helped me turn business ideas into action. The 3 Cs, which represent three phases, are creation, control, and cash flow. They all play off against each other, but for now, we will focus on the creation phase. The creation phase is a critical element of a successful note-investing business, and that's what this book is all about. Recall from *Note Investing Made Easier* that there are four steps to note investing: sourcing, due diligence, asset management, and portfolio management. In the creation phase, you take a step back and put some serious thought into how you can enable each step in a way that aligns with the goals you created in your living financial statement. For example, this might involve budgeting your operating expenditure for acquiring vendor services or considering a monthly passive income goal for yourself.

How should sourcing look if done well? Do you envision an assembly-line approach for due diligence that allows you to vet one note or fifty in a consistent and efficient manner? How can you build systems around asset management to stay compliant and make serious strides with borrowers? The questions you can ask are endless, but your answers will provide solutions that can help you meet the goals laid out in your living financial statement. The more detailed your answers, the better you'll be able to document your systems and standard operating procedures (SOPs). In this chapter, I'll guide you through all of this.

The Creation Phase Explained

The living financial statement will define what your end goals are, but you will only achieve your goals with the right amount of planning and activity. The creation phase is a good starting point to help you move in the right direction. You will develop SOPs during the creation phase that will help you put your creative practices into play and keep your company organized. Later on, we will cover building controls in your operation to increase cash flow.

Form a Vision, a Mission Statement, and Core Values

My mission statement for years was helping homeowners stay in their homes with payments they could afford while making a profit for myself. It's my win-win model. In 2023, however, my investment fund acquired new cash-flowing asset classes and began growing rapidly, encouraging us to revise our vision and mission statements:

Vision: "To be the most trusted and essential global investment firm."

Mission: "To inspire investor confidence by working only with highly talented professionals who acquire and manage quality assets that generate superior returns."

The vision statement is where we see our company going in the next five years or so, and the mission statement is what we will achieve to get there. As a company, we have five core values that define our company and team members. These values are commitment, perseverance, teamwork, results, having fun, and getting results. Every morning we hold a company-wide team meeting that focuses on one of the core values. Monday is commitment day, Tuesday is perseverance day, Wednesday is teamwork day, Thursday is having fun day, and Friday is results day. We start the week with goals we are committed to and end the week with results. We have twenty-plus team members, and each one takes a turn running the meeting. These interactive meetings always have an educational element. For example, one Monday (commitment), James in marketing went around the room and asked everyone what their goals were for the week and asked them to choose an accountability partner to help them meet their goals. How is that for the start of Monday morning? You may have smaller teams, or perhaps you are a one-person show, but you can still begin building out a culture that you would like to see within the company you are building.

Everything I do in note investing goes back to that mission statement. You can be like me and keep your mission statement simple and easy to follow. I highly recommend this. Your mission statement does not need to be convoluted and sound complex or eloquent. It's supposed to be a simple statement about what you're about and what you're trying to accomplish. The bottom line is just to have one before you start.

You have unique experiences that have led you to the point where you're reading this book today. What got you interested in note investing in the first place? What seemed attractive about it? Likewise, why have you chosen to pursue it over the many other investment opportunities? Those sorts of questions are great places to start. You have to do a deep dive into real estate investing even to find note investing. It's a very niche field. Uncovering your reasons for entering it will help you identify your goals and mission.

Deal Flow Is King

Remember when I said that cash and cash flow were not king? Deal flow is king. You may be thinking, "How is that possible?" It may fly in the face of everything you've ever learned from business school, but let's put those things on the shelf for now. Since deal flow occurs in the sourcing stage, you will need a ton of creativity in this area. Image a world where you receive ongoing off-market opportunities where you can negotiate pricing. The competition is just you! Perhaps you are there now, but I can tell you that most aren't. How can you use creativity to set yourself apart from your competition and position yourself to receive ongoing opportunities? For my part, I did this by 1) always keeping my word during trades 2) being an easy trade partner to work with 3) showing up at the right conferences and speaking at many of them 4) writing books and mentoring as a way to give back.

Creation is an ongoing process. It's something that you never stop working on. When working on an early draft of this book, I was flying to a conference trying to collect business cards and generally hoping to extract some good deals on the backend. I coordinated with four of my protégés who were attending with me as well. We were a team of five. We did a lot of legwork before and during the conference whereby we cross-referenced the attendance list with LinkedIn. We conducted a strategy session the day before and worked on our delivery to the players who would be attending, hoping to brand ourselves as a unified front. We even role-played some of our interactions.

Many note investors showed up at that conference, but in most cases, they were one person representing their entire fund or company, whereas we were a team of five. We had five times more exposure than most of the note investors there, which carried significant weight and increased the likelihood of us striking some deals. The end result was we were able to source and acquire a large pool of mortgages from a new buyer we did not know existed.

Writing this book took me through the creation phase as well, forcing me to think of my strategies and new ways of doing things. Through this process, I've realized I tend to look at what is commonplace in the note industry and ask myself how I can do something that's never been done before. In other words, I'm always in creation mode.

Your goal should be to adopt this mindset, asking questions that make you think about your work differently. For instance, put some serious thought into how you currently source deal flow:

- How do you currently rate your performance?
- What is lacking and what can you do differently?
- What is preventing you from making the changes?
- What are you willing to change today?

Asking questions is at the heart of creativity. Don't underestimate them.

Building Your Financial Foundation

Successful note investors do not make excuses often. You rarely hear that external forces are holding them down or that their deal flow is drying up. Those are the words of people who are *not* successful. As you go through the 3 Cs, know that you are cultivating a mindset and building a foundation for your business—one that will serve you for years to come. The following principles can keep you on track and help guide your thinking.

Don't Be a Drifter

When I wrote the first version of this book, I put together a buyer's group that sourced a trade opportunity almost every month. Fast-forward to 2023, I operate a mortgage note fund with my partner that manages around $75 million in mortgages. There are plenty of opportunities out there if you position yourself correctly. Likewise, you can screw it up or grow something mediocre that will not make you proud in the end. Not reaching your full potential rarely comes down to making a few major wrong decisions; usually, it comes down to several small decisions that add up and create drifting. Drifting is when your decisions or habits slowly bring you off course. If you wake up one day and do not understand why your business is the way it is, you likely have been drifting. Drifting usually occurs in the sourcing phase of note investing. You close on a note trade, and the cost-of-capital clock begins to tick. This tends to motivate you to work on getting maximum return for your efforts. You blink, and your deal flow has dried up because you spent all your time asset managing your notes.

Implementing tools such as the living financial statement and working through the 3 Cs can help you avoid this and stay on track with your business.

If you want a better future, then you need to change what you do outside of work. Maybe you are watching too much TV; that time could be better spent on focusing on ways to improve your future.

Successful people have the right habits. When they find success, it's because they've been plugging away and trying things that didn't always work. It didn't happen overnight. They tried and failed often, but they kept pushing and kept the right attitude, and ultimately, things started to break their way. The general public usually doesn't get to see all the hard work that goes into achieving success; they only see the end result. Be wise and recognize that success doesn't come overnight.

Create Your Own Business Model

If you can know where you are starting (i.e., living financial statement) and have a vision of the end point (i.e., vision statement), you can chart a course to get you from point A to point B. There are several ways you can break into the note-investing space or reinvent yourself:

- Bird dogging (sourcing deals for others in exchange for a fee)
- Due diligence support (helping other note investors with their due diligence efforts)
- Asset management services (working out notes for investors for a fee or equity position)
- Full-service note investing (working all four phases of the note-investing process)

- IT solutions (providing custom-build databases, exchange platforms, CRMs, and more for note investors)
- Capital partnerships (investing capital into opportunities)

I based my original model on keeping homeowners in their homes with payments they can afford. I want to keep homeowners happy in their homes, and I do everything possible to achieve that. This informs my entire due diligence process, as I seek the assurance that I can work with borrowers in a meaningful way. You may develop an entirely different model that works for you. Given what you know of the industry at this moment, write down your desired niche and model. This will help you as you go through the creation phase. There may be different ways to achieve this vision, and part of the creation phase involves helping you find a practical, structured, and legal way to do so.

Mind-mapping software, like X-Mind, can help you here. I've been using this software for several years to help me sort through my thoughts. Below is an example of the use:

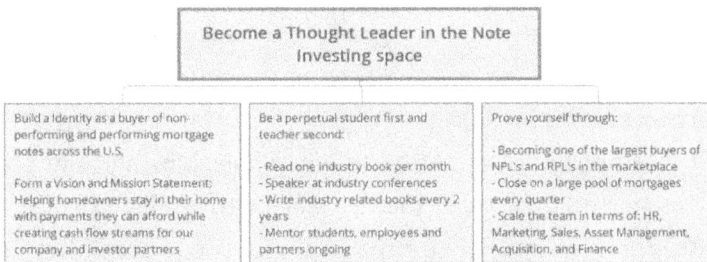

You need to understand what business model works best for you given your financial situation. Each model and exit strategy comes with its own ramifications, but when you find a structure that's a good fit, you can build your sourcing strategy and due diligence SOPs around it. More on all of this in the next chapter

If Bootstrapping, Do It Right

I learned quickly that starting a business and living solely off that income was a scary proposition. It made me mature quickly. After frequent discussions with bankers, I started speaking their language regarding financial responsibility, which is all about credit scores and other factors that indicate credit worthiness. To give my business its best shot, I had to change my habits and improve my financial report card—I needed a larger line of credit to get started.

When my wife and I got started, we took out $225,000 in high-interest credit card debt to buy equipment and get the operation going. We started out of the basement of our home, but we still needed capital. Merely having access to high-interest debt that I had to pay back didn't set me up to be financially responsible.

Being financially responsible is something that no one else does for you. Only you can do that for yourself, and it takes a lot of discipline and hard work. Set goals, adhere to them, and before you know it, you'll see the credit scores going up and the financial reports improving.

It was not until we started to win bigger jobs and the profit margins started to increase that we started to see light behind the clouds. We were pushing to get a healthier line of credit from the bank, and I restructured my whole life around that process. I consolidated all of our credit card debt with a consumer credit service, and I started pounding away at those monthly payments.

Within about two years, we paid off the high-interest debt that had strangled us right out of the gate.

All circumstances are unique, but be prepared. If you are making a run at setting up a note investment company, take the necessary steps to obtain financial health and stability. This is critical. And honestly, it just takes creating and maintaining your living financial statement, updating it, and being smart with your finances. Think of your financial statement and your credit score as your report card, and work with a CPA to stay on track.

No Man Is an Island

The days of note investing solo are long gone. You really need a team, internal or external, to maximize your chances of success. Consider your strengths. That's the value you are bringing to the team. Look at your weaknesses. You are going to need people around you who will offset them.

Your strengths can come in the form of habits, intelligence, or maybe hustle. Maybe you have a background in finance or real estate, or maybe you're a rehabber with a strong sense of what a hard money lender looks at from a credit standpoint. In those cases, you'll face less of a learning curve, which is a major strength.

Strengths can also include your resources like time and access to connections. Document your strengths and resources—at least five. Then list your weaknesses and the resources you lack. Those are opportunities for others on the team to step in.

Find the Right Attorney

To operate in the mortgage note industry, you need a strong creditor rights attorney. In fact, you need a good creditor rights attorney in every state in which you own notes. They will help you with legal matters involving borrowers and collateral and keep you on track with any licensing requirements. With that said, I recommend having a good general counsel you can use for general matters such as contracts, employee matters, agreements, and so on.

If you are brokering deals, you must meet certain licensing requirements. This is why it's so hard to jump into the note space headfirst without the proper education and groundwork. Consult your lawyer on what you need to have as a licensed broker or to operate as a different kind of entity with a different kind of licensure.

Find the Right CPA

When searching for a CPA (because you definitely need one), be sure to ask them whether they understand the concept of note investing. Not all CPAs are familiar with note investing, but you need an expert on your side. To find the right CPA, be sure to take the following steps:

- Ask about their specialization
- Look up their license
- Consider their experience
- Consider their fees
- Ask for client referrals

A great way to find a CPA is through recommendations from current note investors. You can find them through various social media note-investing groups.

I spoke with a CPA Jason Osser, who has extensive knowledge of note investing and happens to be a note investor himself. He has some fantastic tips to help get you started.

Interview with CPA Jason Osser

Martin: What are some of the similarities and differences between the note industry and other industries, Jason?

Jason: The note industry is like most businesses. When you think of the note industry, it's a little bit more than just investing. Think of it more as being a landlord or owning a property; there's a little bit more work involved.

As such, you have to think of that ahead of time. If you started any other business you would have QuickBooks and an accountant, and you would keep good track of records, receipts, expenses, and revenues.

Go with that mindset when you are purchasing notes, particularly because you usually purchase many at one time and you need to be able to carefully track each of those to understand how you're doing.

Martin: What is your recommendation for note investors as they purchase notes? How about when they begin to experience income and expenses on an ongoing basis? How should they keep their books up to date?

Jason: I would treat [for purposes of accounting] note investing like any other business, and we do a lot of work with small business owners on a monthly basis. Because some of the types of notes are nonperforming notes, one of the things you try to do is work with the borrowers to convert them to performing notes.

If you accomplish this, you will now collect a payment on a monthly basis. You will have some expenses that go out, so you really want to set aside some time every month for your business and track how you're doing.

Martin: In regards to a self-tracking system, if they go with Quicken or QuickBooks or something like that, should they still seek out a CPA's help to get them all set up, or can they simply wing it?

Jason: It would be very advisable to speak with a CPA. I do a lot of QuickBooks training to get that set up, as do a lot of other CPAs. You want to have a good familiarity with that, particularly because you need to know how to break down and easily access certain kinds of information.

Martin: What is the importance of working with a CPA who understands the note industry? No two businesses are the same.

Jason: It's kind of like anything else. There are a lot of generalists, and there are a lot of specialists. It's having that extra peace of mind knowing that you're working with someone who understands the ins and outs of this business because note investing is unlike other types of investing.

It leads to other things. I've done note investing, so I know that some of these notes become performing.

On some of these notes, you may be able to get the house back, if you're lucky, and all of a sudden, you're now the landlord, and you own a house. But what are the tax implications of selling a house versus renting a house? It's helpful to work with a CPA or accountant who understands the industry.

Jason is a great resource. Making sure that you consult a CPA like Jason who has knowledge of the note industry is paramount.

After going through some elements from the creation phase and having looked internally and asked some key questions, it's now time to turn to the next step—how to find *your* business model. Let's take a look. There are quite a few questions you will be asking yourself.

NOTE INVESTING FUNDAMENTALS

CHAPTER 3

◆ ◆ ◆

Finding *Your* Business Model

When setting out to determine which business model best suits you, you have several things to consider. First, you'll want to examine what is going on in the marketplace. For instance, you might want to understand what businesses and investors are already established. In addition, you'll want to do some self-reflection on what you've done so far:

- Have you assembled your living financial statement?
- Have you started the creation phase?
- Have you started to build a team that complements your strengths and weaknesses?
- Have you worked on time management?
- Have you formed your vision, mission, and core values?
- Have you vetted and found the right CPA and attorney?

To get your business off the ground, you need to account for your business identity, mechanics, and community. In this chapter, I'll help you account for these three key inputs to help you find the right business model.

Assessing Your Commitment

When considering the right business model, ask yourself the following, "What am I willing to sacrifice?" What you sacrifice is a direct reflection of how much you value yourself.

Next, "What is your level of passion for achieving your goals?"

You will put in more dedication the more that you see you are worth it. When my wife and I started our company, we bought our first home. Then came the 2008 market crash, and we lost 25 percent of our fair market value almost immediately. We drove ten-year-old vehicles that were constantly breaking down on us. Our home needed repairs.

I used to weed whack the lawn because I did not have a lawn mower, and I remember how horrible the lawn would look afterward—how uneven it would be. It was a big day when I was able to buy a new mower.

I remember handing credit cards to the grocery clerk and laughing, telling her, "I hope it goes through, or we're going to have to put the stuff back."

I was working seven days per week with little balance in my life. When I was sleeping, I dreamed about bills coming due and other stressors.

That's why I ask, "What are you willing to sacrifice?" It is true that note investing can result in passive income, but that depends on how you structure your business, and there's nothing passive about what you need to do to get to that point. This is important for you to understand. It takes a lot of work and commitment, maybe a cutback on your expenses, and then also your time.

Identity Runs through All You Do

If I bumped into you on an elevator, could you tell me in a very clear and concise manner and within about ten or twenty seconds what it is that you do for a living?

"I raise capital for a living." Or, "I help people achieve monthly passive income that is consistent and predictable." I can say that within a few seconds, and you understand what it is that I do. Distilling your identity in this way will be key to your business.

Think about your social media profile. The community that you build for yourself is part of your identity. When trying to assess your identity, look at all of those factors. Think about what your identity is and how people view you in the space.

A pitch sheet is a marketing flyer that tells people what your company does, especially your core competencies. When beginning a business, however, creating a pitch sheet is best seen as an opportunity for you to focus your mindset and identify three or so things that you do extremely well. It helps you understand your identity in the note space.

A good pitch sheet clarifies who you are (your bio), your pricing, and things people may be able to work with you on. If your identity is clear and your reputation is trusted, then you will eventually surround yourself with the right people and move forward. Going through the creative phase and having your controls buttoned up will help you form your identity.

Note Investing Is All about the Mechanics

The mechanics of note investing are the day-to-day activities of being a note investor. You need to have your due diligence down pat and set up with all of the vendors so that you can order the reports you need. You should know how to review those reports within your process flow. Then, on the backend, after you make the purchase, you need your project management setup (such as with Microsoft Project or Simplifile).

You also need to get clear on how to manage the collateral file.

Maybe you're using Richmond Monroe scrubbing services or reviewing collateral files yourself. Then, after you acquire the notes, the process by which you communicate and set up legal requests with attorneys will determine the cost of legal and the overall efficiency of the note workout process with the homeowner. As for the borrower outreach portion of note investing, how are you going to work with borrowers to create a win-win scenario whereby you're helping them out with payment terms they can afford while paying off the note and owning the property free and clear?

You will need to get clear on all of the above and input all of your income and expenses on the backend. When I started out, I used QuickBooks for my tracking. I set up my borrowers and recorded all incomes and expenses against each borrower because, at the end of the day, this is its own asset and needs to be treated as such. The expenses are flowing through it.

If you set up your mechanics correctly, your systems and processes will be in line with your mission statement. That's a key goal to keep in mind. You have to take full responsibility for everything that occurs within your business, so if you see something that doesn't resonate with you like a community or a partner or whatever the case may be, then you have the responsibility to make changes. If you don't, then it's completely on you. No excuses.

Community Assures You Are Not Alone

If you watch TV, for instance, you may instead swap that for time connecting with peers in the industry. If you have friends you go out with on the weekends, guess what? You may need to spend less time connecting with them and instead build out your contact list through a good note-investing Facebook group or doing your research on LinkedIn. You will be making new friends, and you may see a drastic reduction in other types of friends as you start to replace them with peers. That's not to say that you cannot have friends outside of work, but there is definitely some commitment that will be required on your part as you conduct your peer outreach and sourcing.

Try to keep in mind that you are starting to grow a new community of friendship with people who are invested in the same goals of financial freedom or freedom of time as you. These are the people who are aligned with your own goals and passions. Their influence will help you to become successful, especially during the tough times when you ask yourself, "Is this worth it?" When I was a government contractor, finding a group of like-minded entrepreneurs I could talk with, commiserate with, and gain encouragement from gave me a vital sense of community.

You need to depend on others in the industry to succeed, but you also must be discerning. You want the highest caliber people around you. Plenty of players will send you note tapes, but if they prove unreliable or keep sending tapes to hundreds of note investors, don't waste your time. Always be pruning your community, and that includes note sellers. Replace the whiners with successful people, and eventually, the community around you will be those who achieve and want success. You'll need that within the note space.

Putting Identity, Mechanics, and Community Together

Each and every week, you should be thinking in terms of all three inputs—your identity, the community, and the mechanics. That should be part of an ongoing self-review. You need to be able to make corrections when necessary, and that means revisiting your action plan every week. As you build your community, you will receive more notes that play well with your mechanics. Identity, mechanics, and community all feed off each other—and that's the point.

Merging the front-end portion of note investing—the sourcing and due diligence—with the backend will allow you to buy more notes, but it creates the need to record and manage those things effectively. You'll want to track metrics to measure your success. This will allow you to adjust where needed, build stronger habits, and carry those forward.

Whenever you see yourself falling short on something, create a game plan to plow through it and adjust. Consider finding a partner who can help compensate for your weaknesses, or perhaps find an accountability partner to ensure you stick to the goals and tasks you set for yourself. When I first started note investing, I was inexperienced. I sourced the notes and performed my own due diligence. I did every single aspect of note investing myself—hundreds of times. Every weakness I had would bubble to the surface, and I had to overcome them. Now that I'm involved in larger trades, the shortcomings I have are even more evident. Fortunately, I have partners who are absolutely amazing, and they pick up any slack that needs to be picked up.

Anytime there's a weakness, just remember that there are also strengths. Tracking your time and the results of each task will help you better assess your strengths and weaknesses. Think about strategic partners who you need to connect with. Also, think about the vendors you need to employ.

There are a number of vendors who will provide you with due diligence reports like property reports, lien searches, and title searches. There are a lot of options, and some of them can do all your due diligence for you. However, know there is a whole art to proper due diligence, so I recommend not being too removed from that process.

There's a lot you can learn about the notes and the opportunity—and the dirtier your hands get—the more successful you will be. With the right plan, you can do this effectively.

Building a Massive Action Plan (MAP)

You've thought a lot about what your business might be, and now it's time to make it happen. In this section, you'll learn how to develop a road map and strategy to plan out your next twelve months. Everything you do will revolve around this plan, which I call the massive action plan (MAP). A MAP is your game plan to get you from point A to point B. Let's say, for example, you want to go from a newbie to someone who owns twenty mortgage notes in one year. To do that, your MAP could be broken out as follows:

- Months 1–3: Produce a living financial statement. Form my mission, vision, and core values. Create a list of vendors and strategic partners I need around me. Throughout the creative phase, develop SOPs I will commit too. Find the right CPA and attorney.
- Months 4–6: Focus on forming the right habits, beginning with the Sourcing Life Cycle (SLC) discussed in *Note Investing Made Easier*. This involves determining my identity (i.e., business model), branding my company, building a conference schedule, starting outreach on LinkedIn, and vetting deals with the vendors I set up in months 1–3.

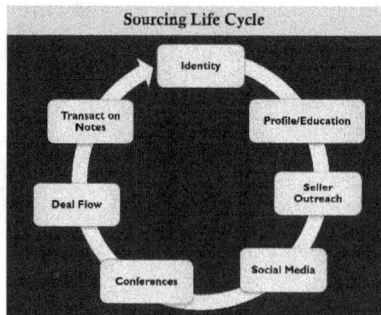

Sourcing Life Cycle

- Months 7–9: Look to close my first note deal. Per the SLC, this will further solidify my identity and improve my reputation. Emphasize developing asset management SOPs to get maximum performance from my investment.
- Months 10–12: As I am working out my first tranche of notes, I need to start the sourcing process again, so I am working on various points of the SLC at the same time.

Your MAP will likely look different from this, and it should. It needs to align with your vision and mission statement. If your vision is to have a mortgage note fund in five years, and your mission is to acquire high-quality notes with capital partners to get there, your MAP should reflect all the activities and timelines needed to achieve your mission.

Start by asking yourself what business model best suits you. What type of business fits *your* character and *your* unique background? You can refer back to some of the popular business models mentioned in chapter 2. You can also look to other sources, as long as you maintain a critical eye. You may have read some books, participated in some social media groups, or watched some webinars. Everyone who has provided you with information or advice on note investing has their own angle and objectives, which is valuable, but they likely provided content to you for a reason. Some already have funds in place. Some are looking for joint-venture partnerships. There are educators out there too, but you must keep in mind that it benefits them to portray themselves as the expert; it is a dynamic that is slanted in their favor, and that is unlikely to change. Often their goal is to perpetually keep you in the mentality that you are a student, not an actual colleague.

These kinds of note investors, however, can help you find your niche. Some need people like you to go out and pick up notes while they provide asset management. In other words, they want to do the work on the backend—to convert the note from nonperforming to performing. You'll have to decide whether that's the model that works best for you. Likewise, passionate educators may suggest you follow their models, but those models may not work for you.

The key is to find your own model. Observe industry players at conferences, online, in webinars, and so on, and write down what you like and do not like about their approaches, models, and results. This will help you form your identity, determine how you would like to be perceived, and create a model that works for you. Furthermore, these connections will give you information on how to improve your mechanics and enhance your community development. Through it all, let your vision, mission, and core values help you determine the best model that works for you.

What Is Your Exit Strategy?

Are you just looking to build a portfolio of loan modifications and take in the monthly payments every month? A few hundred here and there could add up to income that could become quite significant in the future.

Alternatively, are you looking at first-mortgage notes and taking back properties? I learned early on that there are many note investors that buy notes as a back door method to obtain the property. I determined I did not want to do that, but it could be a strategy for you.

Another viable strategy is refreshing or rehabbing so you can flip properties. That's more of a capital gain play where you're looking at large but more sporadic chunks of income. It's a very niche area in its own right, but perhaps that's where your background is strongest.

Whatever the case may be, understanding yourself from the perspective of your exit strategy will help you find your way through the note industry *and* help you make connections moving forward. You will want to home in on individuals with similar strategies and learn from them.

You don't have to know how to take back properties, for example, at this point or even how to do a loan modification with a borrower—right now. You just want to get a level sense of what your exit strategy and objectives are. Once you see what business models are out there, you really just want to see what resonates with you.

Let the Research Guide You

LinkedIn, unlike other social media platforms, is all about sourcing and outreach. It is one of the greatest free resources out there today. I highly recommend you use it and sign up for the sales navigator tier (which you can often get as part of a free trial). It lets you search through and find other note professionals. With that tool, you can better understand the reasoning behind certain company names and how they position and describe themselves in the note space. I would spend hours in that LinkedIn portal doing some research—not so much to connect with others but to understand. Journal about what you find, as this will give you historical data to draw on when needed and give you a timeline of events. It also further reinforces what you are learning and can give you a competitive advantage at times. I've journaled every day for years, and it has paid off. I start each day using the 10X planner and document the following:

- Quote of the day. This is a quote describing how I feel going into the day.
- Targets. These are people and activities I'm going to focus on that will drive me closer to my goals.
- Goals. These are my short-term and long-term goals. For example, as I write this book today, my goals are: 1) be the spiritual leader for my family, 2) be in top shape physically, mentally, spiritually, and emotionally, 3) be loving and kind to my family and myself, and 4) achieve my work goals.
- My agenda for the day, hour by hour.
- Tasks I have to accomplish each day. I cross them off as I achieve them and place a star next to the item that will carry over to the next day.

Combining journaling with regular industry research will give you an edge over those who don't. Who knows—you may find someone who inspires you. If you look at a hundred profiles in our industry, you will find maybe five or six people whom you wish to become or emulate. Imitation is the sincerest form of flattery, and there is no shame in using someone's business model for yourself. Nobody has a patent or trademark on that. Obviously, if you want to use their description, you'll want to rewrite it for you and make it more about you, but seeing how someone describes themselves and their company might help you figure out what works best for you. In the end, you have to build processes around documenting and processing the information you are obtaining.

The images on the following pages are snapshots of what you can find on LinkedIn with the LinkedIn Sales Navigator.

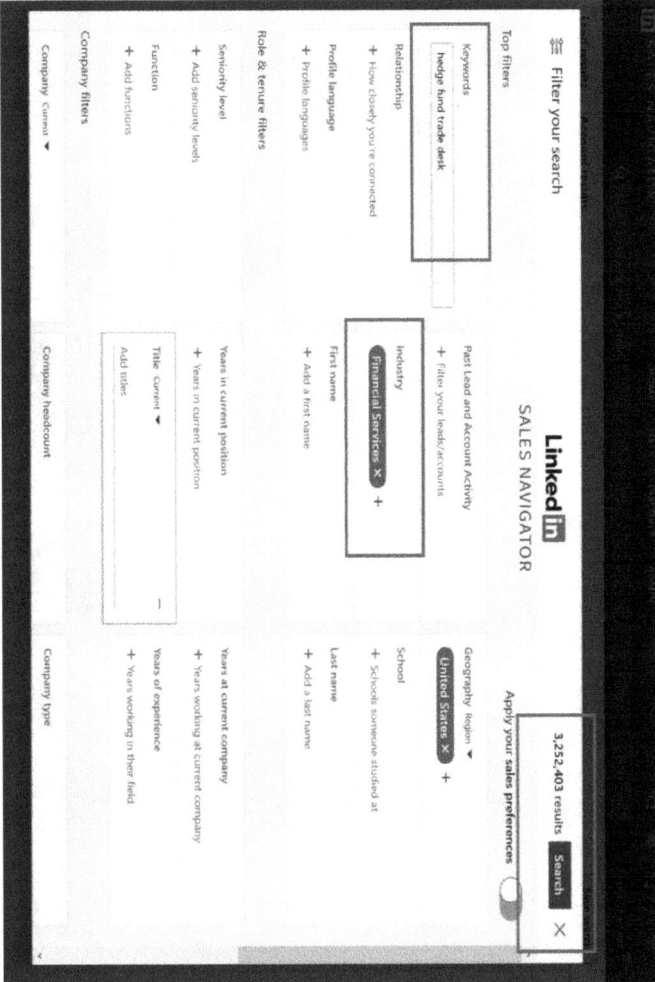

You're going to want to develop a business model for yourself based on whatever resources you already have. You've already listed out your resources like education, time, capital, and so on. As you find people you resonate with on LinkedIn, you may notice you already have the resources available to do what they're doing. You may notice you have a similar background or other strengths to do what they're doing, as well. You might be closer to succeeding like them than you think, or you'll have a better idea of the resources you need to acquire or compensate for building a business like theirs. In the latter case, perhaps their kind of business is a long-term goal to strive for after you reach a more achievable short-term goal. This is a pivotal moment as you craft a business model that makes sense for you based on your own resources and strengths. Where you find yourself lacking, you can bring in strategic partners.

So that's what LinkedIn looks like. With Facebook, however, I advise you to be very careful. In 2013, Facebook was a very different space—it was more casual, informative, and expressive. It was a place where we would just come together as a note community and help each other out. We would celebrate each other's successes. We would be supportive of each other. That's not the case anymore. Now, there's just a lot of boasting.

There are a lot of people out there with flashy ads and phrases. There is a dizzying array of clickbait. These individuals and ads are on there to funnel you into whatever program they're pushing and trying to ultimately upsell. Rather than being a productive place, Facebook offers a lot of background noise. I haven't been on Facebook since 2020 for this very reason. You can navigate LinkedIn much easier without all of the distractions. It's more for businesspeople; it's also a great place to start building a network of peers for yourself.

Let Research Enhance Your MAP

To build your MAP, you will be placing events on a timeline. Map out everything that you need to do to make your plan a reality in the next twelve months. One suggestion is to stop where you're at in the book, right now, and draw a blank timeline; then, as you start reading along, you can fill in the timeline based on the points I make. Include a self-reflection stage as part of that timeline. That should be a very critical first part of your new note business. This is an example of an X-Mind MAP for the first three months of a note investor's career:

Mind mapping can be an excellent tool to help you organize your MAP. You can break out different categories of activities, which may help you structure your thoughts. In this example, you see that the focus in the first three months of note investing is to get a handle on finances, develop a marketing strategy, get a sourcing plan in place, and start assembling due diligence systems. This document will be living so you can easily update it as needed (essentially focusing on the three inputs of identity, mechanics, and community).

It's not going to be a perfect action plan. You might not be able to capture all of the steps. There's so much you don't know at this point. At least get a roadmap started and put down all of the steps as you learn them. It is a living timeline that you'll be updating on an ongoing basis. You can add steps or revise existing ones as you learn better ways of doing things.

Heed My Words—Do Not Let Someone Crap on Your MAP!

There is something to be said about being creative and building your own course into note investing; however, it can help to have some mile markers in place.

You may take someone's overall advice, but at the end of the day, your model needs to be tightly connected to you and your belief systems. If you follow quick-fix roadmaps, their creators are selling you something that you will most likely have no passion for, leaving you worse off than you are right now.

This is why I implore you to make a MAP for yourself. Leverage what others are out there doing in the note space right now; that is a good start. A better one is befriending a note investor to review your MAP with you. You can see whether they have any kind of advice on the subject that could be valuable for you. Your roadmap and plan are something you'll be working on on an ongoing basis.

Broadcasting Your Identity

In the beginning, when you are operating on a shoestring budget, you are going to want to monitor your spending tightly. By all means, eat cheap! Be frugal! People often find themselves spinning their wheels and spending a lot of money, and they end up making many mistakes. They don't have action partners that hold them accountable. They don't have buddies to help them.

But being cheap can be a deathblow for your new note business if you aren't careful. You should absolutely be frugal and understand where every dollar of your money is going and know what value you are getting in return for those dollars. There is much to be said about bootstrapping a new venture. It can force you to be creative and put in the work—but this is not the same thing as being cheap.

As for spending money, here are areas where you should consider your money well spent:

- Hiring someone for your brand and marketing campaign
- Attending industry conferences
- Getting a Sales Navigator subscription on LinkedIn
- Setting up with all the vendors needed for due diligence (RealtyTrac, Credco, Lexus Nexus, PACER, ProTitle USA, etc.)
- Hiring competent creditor rights attorneys
- CRM services and potential customization of software

The last thing you need is to start a business and get a negative label because you are not equipped to operate at expected levels. Something like that will carry on through your note-investing business and follow you. People in the note space are independent, and if they don't like you, they will avoid you like the plague.

Identity and branding must look consistent from the outside. You have done self-reflection and research, but now it's time to research yourself. Ask yourself the following questions:

- "What does your social media presence look like?"
- "How's your profile on LinkedIn?"
- "How do you describe yourself?"

- "How do you show yourself on Facebook and other social media outlets?"
- "What is your company name?"
- "Do you have a mission statement?"

At this point, think back to the SLC and all the phases involved and how you can button up your approach in each area.

All of these things are important.

Social Media Services a Place

You need your social media to reflect who you want to portray yourself as in your note business. Ask your friends and family members to give you their impression of your social media so you can get a sense of whether you've hit the mark. Ask them, "What do you think my page says about me?"

With honest feedback from people that you trust, you can better understand how you're presenting yourself and determine whether it's in line with your objectives as a note investor. Journaling will help store all of this daily information intake so you can process it in a way that will give you an advantage.

Choosing a Company Name

Your brand should speak directly to whoever is putting money or notes directly into your pocket. This is a big area where I see a lot of note investors getting things wrong. They have a company name and pitch sheets, but they do not speak to the person who is putting money in their pocket. When I wrote the first edition of this book, my company name was "2nd Chance Funding," and my target audience was borrowers. They see they are being offered a second chance and that I am all about helping homeowners stay in their homes with payments they can afford. The homeowners are the ones who are putting money directly in my pocket, so the branding is meant for them.

Whatever you do, speak well of and present well to the people who are compensating you. If you keep that in mind, you will make a lot of money in this space.

Look at your company name, logo, business cards, and job title. These are the key places for branding. You can be creative with it. Think again about LinkedIn. As long as everything that you do speaks to you as a note investor, most industry professionals won't look poorly at you if you have a nine-to-five job while setting up your note business. Strategic partners will just want to know you can handle the work and deliver results. In terms of a title, go with something like, "Bookkeeper/Note Investor." It's OK to mix it up.

If you're buying notes, and your business model is to work with borrowers and buy notes, then you'll want them to find you on LinkedIn. However, if you're model is more of an advisory service, and you're matching buyers with sellers or offering consulting services, then the person putting money in your pocket is the note buyer. They are paying your fee for sourcing their notes. At the end of the day, your company name (and ergo, business cards and logo) must speak to who is compensating you.

Pay Attention to Areas of Improvement

Everyone has areas they can improve on. The challenge is that if you are new to an industry, you may now know enough to understand the shortcomings of people around you. That is why it is essential you become a student of the note industry and connect with as many people as possible. That will fast-track you toward the work you do best. Do note, however, that someone's weaknesses may not present themselves right off the bat, so stay guarded as you navigate the community. I've mentored numerous people, and from that experience, I've found it takes a month or so for weaknesses to come out. The same is true of a business model.

One weakness that sometimes rears its ugly head is procrastination. As weaknesses appear, you have to decide whether you want to address them or compensate for them in some way (e.g., through an internal or external partner or a virtual assistant or whatever the case).

Some other common weaknesses seen in the industry are:

- No dedicated effort or game plan for sourcing deal flow on a regular basis.
- Not having branding tight. All your branded marketing material needs to look uniform and speak well to your vision and mission for your company.
- Lack of technical skills to perform adequate due diligence. Just because someone is great at drumming up a note opportunity does not mean that person should run the opportunity through the due diligence process.
- Running asset management without a compliance gameplan in place. You'll need to follow federal and state licensing requirements. Even certain cities have licensing requirements. It is your job as a note investor to work closely with your attorney to be and stay compliant.

The Marketplace Will Reward Your Strengths If You Address Your Weaknesses

Likewise, your strengths will come out as you get into a groove and start doing well. You will know exactly what your strengths are as you settle in and start doing well. They will expose themselves.

Having a twelve-month plan will help you stay focused on the prize, which will become clearer the closer you get to it. Stay on the course and adapt when needed.

CHAPTER 4

◆ ◆ ◆

Mentorship Comes in Many Forms

If you're struggling to analyze your strengths and weaknesses and set up your own note business, you may benefit from a mentor who can help you evolve into the successful note investor you wish to become. He or she can help you overcome or bypass your weaknesses and can help you determine the value you bring to the marketplace. But a mentor won't do the work for you, of course. The more you have your house in order—from having a living financial statement, a MAP, and a commitment to employing the 3 Cs throughout the process—the better candidate you will be for mentorship.

Recall that I claimed deal flow is king and that deal flow comes from doing a series of steps correctly. A mentor can help you master each step and focus on the habits you need to create and the knowledge you need to acquire so you can enact each step effectively. If you play the game right, all of that will eventually lead to freedom of time or a different overarching goal you have set. Knowing your desired outcome and your processes will allow your mentor to help you get there.

A mentor can help uncover your strengths as you grow. Sometimes they see things in you better than you see them yourself. Honest self-evaluation is difficult. They may notice ways you could correct your course or alter your approach to leverage the strengths you deliver to the market. For example, if you have a likable and genuine personality, your mentor might highlight that as a strength. They know you make great impressions on people, so they might suggest you step away from the day-to-day operations of the note business and instead focus on building relationships with key sellers in the industry.

Maybe you are on the other side of the spectrum and are a bit shy. Perhaps you are building a note-investing business where you do everything in-house, including vetting and asset management. Sometimes your shyness leads to procrastination when it comes time to pick up the phone and make connections. You end up just spinning your wheels, and you don't get anywhere. It's easy to feel stuck here, but a mentor can draw out and acknowledge your strengths. For instance, maybe you have a passion for doing research, a talent for vetting notes as you're purchasing them, and a genuine desire to help people get back on their feet financially. A good mentor will notice this and suggest you partner with or hire someone to work on the front end and help you get the proper deal flow.

The right mentors can help you develop your strengths and minimize your weaknesses. I've mentored several introverted note investors who didn't care for too much interaction with people they didn't know. To help soften the anxiety of talking to people they didn't know, I had them do research on who they would be speaking with and roleplay those conversations so they would feel more comfortable with what would be discussed.

To give you a better sense of what the mentor-mentee relationship looks like, I'll speak from my own experience. When I wrote the original version of this book, I ran a successful note-investing mentorship program, where I mentored employees, educated investors, and acquired new assets. I took on a limited number of one-on-one protégés. We would talk about everything they did the week prior and discuss what they were focused on that current week. I'd help them with everything from the branding phase to setting up a note business for themselves and connecting them with deal flow. When they got some notes in the door, we worked on the actual mechanics of note investing.

They found this sort of hands-on help wildly helpful, but part of that was because they knew I had a focus. My training academy focused on helping individuals buy and profit from distressed mortgage notes. When searching for a mentor, try to find someone who can help with your specific business model. Find someone who has resources that can benefit you. I put my protégés in a buyer's group. I held live workshops. I connected them with strategic partners. A good mentor will see you as more than a student; they want to help you succeed. My mantra was consistent at that time: "I am about creating colleagues, one student at a time." Everything that I did from a training standpoint went back to that mantra. Find someone with that kind of dedication.

Buyer's Groups

Some mentors will help set up opportunities for their protégés, and one of the best of these is a buyer's group. Here, mentees become colleagues and work through deal flow and other aspects of investing over a set period, usually six months. When I set up buyer's groups for my mentees, they worked as follows:

- The person who brought the deal to the table got to run point on it. This will give them experience in project management, buyer communication, contracts, and being a closer.
- We would meet collectively as a group, and the point person would review the opportunity with the group.
- From there, the point person would delegate responsibilities and deliverables to each member.
- The point person would initiate calls after deliverables were due so the team could review the work that had been done collectively.
- If we went forth with a bid, we would build a pricing matrix and determine how much to offer for each note individually based on where it fell within the matrix.

Anyone could bring a deal to the table, but a point person was not required to bring everyone on to a deal. This created a "giver's gain" system that incentivized participation. The more you drove value to the group (usually by bringing deals to the table), the more others would seek to include you in their own deal flow opportunities.

The protégés had an instant community, and they supported each other and provided outside deal flow. They shared the best practices they'd learned, which helped everyone.

Research Potential Mentors

If you're interested in a mentorship, do your research. Before I ever bought a note, I read a dozen or more books on the subject to understand how typical mentorship dynamics are. I caution against group mentorship versus one-on-one mentorship. Most large group mentorships tend to give you a watered-down effect. It's like when you're in middle school and don't get all of the attention you might require. Sometimes you get buried, and you're not getting that one-on-one attention that you need. It's just hard to build a customized business model for yourself when you're in a group setting.

Seek out a one-on-one mentor for optimal support; otherwise, you might be falling down the path of getting a ready-made, prefabricated business model handed to you, which is something to avoid.

My Mentors

When I started in the note industry, Marty Granoff proved an invaluable mentor. I still do deals with Marty. But I've had a host of mentors beyond Marty. Sometimes mentors mentor each other by being accountability partners. Mentors have been essential to my success, and I implore you to get some mentors in your life.

They may be authors, podcast hosts, conference panelists, or paid mentors. I met Marty when I sold him a business note. He taught me his due diligence process by taking me through it as a client. Over time, I sold him performing mortgage notes and further learned how he operated his business.

You can also find mentors at conferences and note-investing events. I met Steve Lloyd in 2013 at a note-investing event next to the Philadelphia airport. He was manning a booth at the time, and I remember being so fascinated by his knowledge of the note space.

"Call me anytime," he said as he handed me his business card. "I want to hear back from you." I noticed his cell phone number on the card and then asked the obvious question.

"Why do you give your cell phone number out? You must get a lot of phone calls?"

"Hardly anyone ever calls me," he replied. That says a lot about people in general: very few people really want help.

Steve is a mastermind in this field. He is highly successful as a landlord, note investor, and lender, and he has mentored me and many others to elevate our businesses.

Despite all of his success, he still loves to give back, and that's an opportunity that one cannot take for granted.

He taught me that you could have ethics, and a huge heart, and still be highly successful at the same time in the note industry. Those things are not mutually exclusive. Not everyone in the note space operates that way, so you will want to be careful.

In one of Steve's mastermind sessions, I cried three times in one day having heard his story. Through it, I learned many valuable lessons about how to break into the note industry, which is why

I've included an interview where Steve shares his story in his own words. I hope his story of success resonates with you as it did with me.

Interview with Steve Lloyd

Steve: Our company [Stone Bay Holdings] is a fund. We ran it through a private placement memorandum. We only raise money from accredited investors. It is based on our three pillars.

First, we buy reperforming and nonperforming notes.

Second, we lend money to investors who might be doing sales, rehabbing, or bridge loans for apartment building guys, for example.

Third, we buy apartment buildings, generally over $20 million. We really don't look at anything under $20 million. Our sweet spot is from $20 million to $60 million. Those are the three pillars. Those are the three asset classes we deal with.

One thing we do that no one else does is put those three asset classes under one fund. There are hundreds of individuals with funds, but they only concentrate that fund on one thing. That one thing might be apartment buildings or lending money or whatever the case may be. They may also buy notes.

Martin: Steve mentions something powerful here. He developed a mastery over three different asset pillars. All involve real estate: notes, private money lending, and multifamily apartments. This allowed his company to move between pillars to find the best deals while still remaining within the real estate umbrella.

Steve: I saw, for me, that buying bulk notes in the $6 million and $7 million range was expensive, so I moved to lending money. That was great for us because it gave us a second pillar. I was able to lend out money. If one pillar is slow, then I can do another, and vice versa. Our fund is a beast of investments in cash flow.

The next part of that relates to why we are different. Someone called me earlier. He asked whether I would come evaluate an apartment building with him. I told him I would, but that I had never evaluated an apartment building. He was at a loss. He asked me how that could be because I own about twelve of them.

I'm a money guy, Martin. So that's what I told him. I had other hacks too. I stopped looking for notes and apartment buildings and began focusing on creating strategic partnerships.

These friends are already very well established when they call me, so when we get together, things really take off. Another guy I work with flips in the $7 million range. He's already good at what he does, but I took it to another level. He was able to make even more deals, for example. He didn't need me to be successful, but it took him to a whole other level. It also helped me, Martin.

Some of these guys can't raise capital. They are experts and good at what they are doing, but they just can't seem to raise capital. I can come in and take them to another level. And it brings me to another level in the process where the pools they buy are much larger now. There are really two things, then, that set us apart—and those are the strategic partnerships and the three pillars. It's incredible for us. It's raining green.

The relationships I have with people in business are what I simply call "culture." At Stone Bay, we've built a culture like no other. When things are good, it's great. But when things got tough, no one left. Everyone still believed in the foundation of the company, and that's where you build culture and belief and know that the company is going to be there for you.

Martin: Steve emphasizes strategic partners as a key to his success. Matching strengths and offsetting weaknesses through partnerships is not just a practice but part of his company's fabric.

Steve: One of the things I'm most proud of is the big party we throw around the holidays. There are about 200 people there, and I will be expecting about 235 people next time. It's the weirdest party ever. Everyone is smiling and hugging, and everyone knows each other's names. It's probably one of the highlights of my entire life having that party for six hours just to give thanks and be grateful and show appreciation to the investors.

That's where so many people go wrong. A big part of what we do is take care of people's money. When someone invests with us, we send them a great gift. We call and thank them again. We talk throughout the year to give them updates. I create friendships. I'm not the business owner. It's really like, "Hey, let me call my friend."

You have to remember that these people are giving you their retirement money, money to buy a second home, or money that could be going to their kid's education or their kid's first home. You have to respect that. Not everything always goes right. The past five years have been great, but it hasn't always been that way. Before Stone Bay, I struggled.

There was always good communication. It wasn't that for me. That's where things tend to go wrong with some people.

When things go poorly, it's often due to a complete communication breakdown and/or loss of respect. The people I work with don't mind if things go wrong. They just want to know how we are going to fix it. That's the key.

Of everything, that is probably the thing that I am most proud of—the relationships I have built with people and the fact we don't make excuses. We formed about seven years ago. We control, between all three pillars, right around $200 million in assets. With all of that in place and all of the oversight needed, we still try to have a presence on social media and give back.

This all stems from the fact that I was raised by my mom and my aunt. Ten and fifteen years ago, those kinds of people were there for me; that's something you don't forget about. Later on, I had to weed a few people out of my life. They will kill your growth.

Martin: Knowing Steve over ten years now and watching him grow his fund and overall success, I know much of his success comes from how he treats people. He has a giving heart and helps people with whatever they are experiencing (i.e., relationships, finance, business ideas, etc.).

Martin: Can you tell us how Stone Bay was born?

Steve: So, I helped to fund big note trades for some large players, and they paid me back with performer mortgages.

I basically did that with three other companies as well, and that's why you don't burn any bridges. I ended up with millions of dollars in reperformers and nonperformers. For Stone Bay, there hasn't been a quarter when we were not profitable. Now, if you go back further to some point in my business career, I had a down point or dip in activity, and there were some problems with associates. I didn't know whether I was going to make it or not.

When people come to me and say they're going to quit their jobs and go into the note world, I tell them to slow down. Don't do anything drastic. Everything in life is about leverage. Start by hanging out with Martin Saenz and others in the note world. That's what is great about the note world.

You are sitting at a desk dealing with this paper. You may have six or seven loans, and you can get a good feel without quitting your job. Once you sell off one or two and get a better feel for it, get one performing, get some cash flow, and feel comfortable, then quit your job.

At that point, go to the next level. I always tell people, when I'm mentoring them, to think about fear.

Think about all of those times you thought you were going to have this crazy problem—you were going to go under or whatever—and it didn't happen. It never happens. It comes down to what you want and how badly you want it and believe in yourself and make it happen. Look at yourself in the mirror. If you want to be that entrepreneur, you have to conquer that fear.

To your readers, I say, set this book down. Cross out the word *fear* and write the word *belief* down instead! One fear is education or background. I would tell people struggling with that fear to talk to a mentor and surround yourself with the right people, but don't let that hold you back. I have no college degree and didn't finish high school, but even so, I manage $200 million in assets. A lack of education doesn't have to hold you back. There's no difference between sitting in an algebra class and a self-directed IRA class. There's a learning curve in one class, the same as the other.

I had no desire to sit in algebra or chemistry. I couldn't care less about that stuff. I wanted to know how I could get compound interest in a Roth IRA and create wealth with my money. That interested me. If you come into this business, you have to put your time in and study and learn. You have to surround yourself with the right people and get that knowledge and have that belief, and the rest will take care of itself. As far as the future of Stone Bay is concerned, we are a phenomenal company. We are going to go wherever the market takes us. We have created a lot of wealth, and my partner and I do some self-funding ourselves.

We may initiate an exit strategy from there in seven or eight years and pay back all of our investors. But we're going to create more strategic partners in the meantime. I'm also going to look at that fourth pillar. It might be cryptocurrency. I don't know what it will be, but there will ultimately be a fourth pillar for us, another stream of income. I believe in diversity, and I like to be consistent because consistent returns, over a long period of time, create wealth.

Martin: Steve hits well on his exit strategy and speaks to having a MAP.

Steve: I have guys that come at me with all kinds of ideas, and it's easy to get lured into some of those. But one piece of advice I can give your readers is to stick to what you know.

Don't be fooled by every charlatan that comes by.

Martin, I once had someone who owned a wood company come to me. He's very successful and built his company from nothing, but he decided he was going to divert all of that and start a distribution line down in North Carolina. I asked him why he would do that; he said he wanted to go bigger. The problem is, you can go bigger without changing or diverting what made you successful in the first place. I think where a lot of people fail is that once they start to do pretty well, they start looking at other things.

I am a hardcore believer in concentrating on what I do best, so that's what we do. I understand that some people start to feel things growing stale. They really just need to find people who can give them new ideas and generate new energy in their business. It's the greatest saying in the world: You are who you hang out with. I watch who I spend my time with for that reason. If you hang out with me, I'm always looking at what value you bring me.

Martin: Staying focused on your core competencies helps you avoid drifting. Again, drifting is not something that occurs overnight, but it is the little shifts in focus that add up over time to something monumental.

Steve: I want to go hang out with the Chip Leavers of the world and people like that. I can't ask them to mentor me. I have to bring something to the table. I have to look at relationships in terms of the mutual benefit. I also gravitate toward people who are always trying to improve, like you. Relationships are all about fair and equal exchange in that regard. A lot of people give me excuses about why they can't have success and bring up past failures and problems. The fact is, you can give all the excuses in the world, but you still have to be accountable.

Be accountable to yourself too. Make your life good and let the joy and happiness flow over to everything else. If you're a leader, people will want to follow you. You can't follow. You must lead. As the saying goes, fill your cup up first, and then it will overflow to everyone else. That's what I do.

I lead by example and try to build the best businesses, and because of that, a lot of people want to run with me. The thing is, though, we can do that, but we're not going to sit or walk together. We're going to run together! Make 100 percent sure that the people you're surrounding yourself with have full confidence they are trying to help you.

Make sure they care about you and your family and want to help you succeed. Sometimes the closest people to us, especially in this business, really are not looking out for our best interest. I look at the twelve guys I deal with today; I know ten of them are pushing me to be better. They ask me what I need versus what they need. It's very important to surround yourself with great people. It's not about who succeeds first. It's about rising that tide together. It's about growing and being successful together, and that's what a lot of people lack.

Martin: The notion that we should work on building ourselves up and then carefully vetting any and all strategic partnerships is key. Steve never jumps into business with anyone. He first carefully observes them on social media for at least six months and does other kinds of background research to understand the character of the individual before entertaining doing any business with them. But keep in mind that you and your mission need to be clearly defined so you can best evaluate partners.

Steve: A great place to start, for your readers, would be taking on a mentor. In that mentor-protégé relationship, your strengths will be maximized, and your weaknesses compensated for.

You may begin by developing a strategic action plan and then start putting the proper controls in place. There's no limit to what can be done once you take the right steps. Make today the best day ever because you will never get it back!

Moving beyond Fear

Steve talked about fear—that we are to strike that word from our vocabulary and use *belief* instead. As you consider becoming a mentor, don't let fear of that new relationship stop you. Don't let fear stop you in general.

Write down the fears you have related to starting your own business. Think about those fears as you move forward.

Next, look at your passion, which can override your fears in powerful ways. Just like Steve, the investment pillars of my income fund were born from my passion for real estate. The cash flow the fund creates each and every month fuels that passion. I can control the asset from the point of purchase and have predictability around the monthly passive income outcome. Think about your passion and your desired outcome, and take time to complete this paragraph:

I am passionate about this area of investing because
_____. It
will allow me to
_____. I plan on
growing my investment in this asset into
_____
_____ by _____. I'm going to
accomplish this through the following steps:
1)_____
2) _____
3) _____
4) _____

If you fill in the blanks with what is truly in your heart, it should spark some passion inside you. If so, perhaps print it out and place it in visible places so you can be reminded of what you are about and where you are headed. In the next chapter, we'll build on all you've learned thus far to help you build controls that make those fears irrelevant.

Part 2: The Control Phase

CHAPTER 5

◆ ◆ ◆

Placing Controls on Sourcing

3 C's of Business

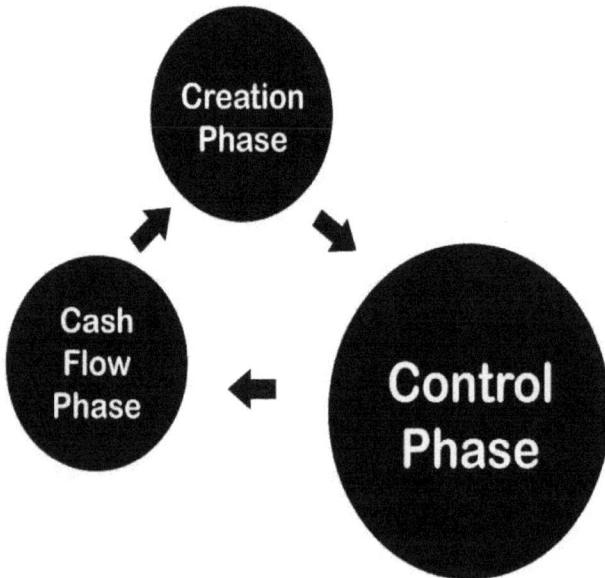

Y ou have done some important self-reflection up to this point, and we've talked about how the creation phase should be part of everything you do. Now, let's discuss the second C—the control phase. This is all about putting the right systems in place to help you manage your successful new note business. Now, just as we discussed running the creation phase in each of the note-investing phases (i.e., sourcing, due diligence, asset management, portfolio management) to find new and better ways to stand out in the industry, you will do the same for the control phase. Let us start by building controls around sourcing because nothing happens until you source deal flow. Deal flow is king!

No matter what your business model, no matter where you're at in your career, putting the right systems in place when it comes to sourcing is crucial. How many business owners do you know that are competent in their product or service offering but fall short when it comes to developing new clients or opportunities? Probably too many.

Even Sourcing Needs Controls

To control sourcing and provide predictability in income, you need defined, measurable steps. In this section, I cover four steps you should follow when building your sourcing strategy. The steps are as follows:

- Step 1: Set up a CRM
- Step 2: Build an outreach matrix
- Step 3: Do the research
- Step 4: Make the phone calls

Step 1: Set Up a CRM

A customer relationship management system (CRM) captures information about whoever you're working with. You want to capture their information and look for opportunities as the notes are released. Even if you aren't tech savvy, creating a CRM system is quite simple. Don't let it scare you. Here is a simple CRM system you can construct in Excel in a matter of minutes. I should know as this is what I used for many years.

First Name	Last Name	Company	Phone#	Email	Notes
Jon	Show	North Funding	888-GET-WILD	Jon@IFOUNDFREEDOM.fun	Understands the note biz and has capital. Seeking someone to source deal flow and would be open to partnership opportuntiy

Strategic Partners	Peers	Hedge Funds	**Capital Partners**	Vendors	⊕

People in your CRM likely include institutional sellers (people who everyone knows about) and various fund managers and tradespeople you want to connect with. Anytime they have a selloff with notes, you'll be included in that opportunity if you've put in the work to build the relationships. Your CRM may even include peers—colleagues in the note space that you want to remain in contact with and build further relationships with. By building out your CRM, you can better offset your weaknesses with strategic partners and develop prospects on an ongoing basis. To do that, you'll want to capture information as you move through this process, and again, that's all part of the systems you put in place.

If you'd like a little more structure behind your Excel spreadsheet CRM, try some free options like Zoho and HubSpot.

Step 2: Build an Outreach Matrix

As you focus on outreach, an outreach matrix will keep you on task and provide you structure on a weekly basis. Essentially, it's an accountability system where you set goals for the week and record whether you met them or not. An example matrix appears below.

NOTE SELLER OUTREACH MATRIX						
	WEEK OF 4/16		WEEK OF 4/23		WEEK OF 4/30	
	GOAL	ACTUAL	GOAL	ACTUAL	GOAL	ACTUAL
RESEARCH	90 mins	45	90 mins		90 mins	
PHONE CALLS	20 CALLS		20 CALLS		20 CALLS	
TAPES VIEWED	1		1		1	
PEER OUTREACH	2		2		2	

You can build a simple matrix like this in Excel, and that's really all you need. Each row represents your outreach activity, and the columns show your goals and actual actions over a series of weeks. For instance, if you want to contact trade desks at hedge funds, you will add that outreach activity to your spreadsheet. Then you'd set your weekly goal. As you work through the week, record your actual results at the end of each day to make sure you're working toward achieving those goals. When you succeed, you'll have a record of that success.

If your deal flow slows down, you either need to step up your outreach efforts, tweak your delivery, adjust your branding, or do something along those lines. Do actions that provide measurable markers of success. Ask yourself some questions. Continue to reflect. As a result of doing all of these tasks, are you hitting your outreach goals?

Procrastination will kill your note business, but the CRM and outreach matrix will help you stay on top of important tasks. It's pretty simple to use once you get the hang of it, and a mentor or colleague can certainly help in this regard. Ideally, this sort of tracking becomes an ingrained habit.

When I did mortgage sales in the 1990s, I used a state-of-the-art CRM system: stapling business cards to a blank sheet of paper. I made phone calls. I took handwritten notes. I set up all of my calls for the next day and kept track of upcoming meetings and that sort of thing. Though simple, it allowed me to become one of the most successful loan officers in a company with seven hundred loan officers.

Step 3: Do the Research

As already discussed, do plenty of research on LinkedIn. As you find people you should be connecting with, you should be capturing their information in your CRM. Doing this should be one of your outreach matrix objectives.

The worst way to navigate LinkedIn is to go in and do a bunch of research without writing down your findings. Then you have to go back and do it all over again. Start building your CRM system from day one. As you do your research, put those people in your CRM system. Think of your CRM as another form of journaling you're finding and processing the data in a way that will bring you closer to having the note business you seek.

Step 4: Make the Phone Calls

This activity is simple. Make phone calls, drive deal flow, make further connections with the folks you are contacting, update your CRM system, and update your outreach matrix. For example, one of my protégés is going to be attending the note conference in Chicago. He will be spending about sixty days researching who's going to be at the conference, cross-referencing those names on LinkedIn, making LinkedIn connections, calling those individuals, and starting to build a rapport with them before the conference. That way, when he goes into the conference, he's more established from day one. Although he's new to the note business, this additional work ahead of time shows he is serious. He will go to the note conference and be honest about being new, but it won't deter people from connecting with and doing deals with him.

This kind of tactic might work for you. You can let others know that you've been in the note-investing space for six months. You've been sourcing a lot of deal flow lately and are at this conference looking for partners to connect with to that end. It's straightforward, honest, and sincere. If you come across something like that, you will get plenty of attention. You will find more deal flow as long as you are genuine and come off as committed to the industry. Everyone's ears perk open when you're mentioning "sourcing" and "deal flow" and things like that. As stated earlier, it's easy to get a bad reputation in the note space by being cheap. As you make the calls, protect your image. You don't want to become persona non grata. Remember, it's all about making connections—and sometimes, even friendships, which, ultimately, will lead to better deal flow. That's the name of the game. Be genuine. The reputation will fall right in place.

If you pick the right conference and plan well, you can find all the players you need to execute your business model by locking down capital partners and matching those partnerships to new deal flow drummed up at the conference. I am writing this from firsthand experience. However, even if you're building your outreach matrix and going to conferences—which is fantastic—you still need to pick up the damn phone and call people! This is very much a phone-call-heavy industry, and it's what makes those conferences work.

Everyone who comes into this space needs to become comfortable and experienced with phone outreach, even if you're not planning on doing that aspect of the business for long. You still need to know what is involved in that aspect of the business.

These sorts of calls can be hard when you don't have the experience and you're surrounded by a bunch of big players; it can be intimidating and maybe even a blow to your self-confidence. Many questions come to mind.

"What do I say?"

"Will I come off sounding like an idiot?"

These are valid concerns, and you may want to get an action partner you meet with weekly and roleplay phone calls so you can start building confidence in this tactic, especially if it's one of your weaknesses. Offer to do some diligence for another investor if that's your strength in return for doing some role-playing, ironing out your weaknesses and overcoming your shyness. Having mentored other note investors, I have seen time and time again that consistent outreach to generate deal flow is a major challenge for many in the space. That applies to veteran investors too. As a result, many investors are left scrabbling for more deal flow after spending a lot of their energy on asset managing the notes from the prior trade win. Pick up the damn phone!

Many investors fall asleep at the wheel, and they gloss over these steps, and it shows in their results.

How We Do It at Bequest

At Bequest, we are set up with a full marketing and sales team. Even though this company is likely far larger than what you'll be building initially, we still employ these four steps in our outreach campaign (CRM, outreach matrix, research, and making calls). That's how important they are. We customized HubSpot so that it handles a full marketing campaign along with it being a sales tool. We have carefully adjusted all the fields in the CRM to fit our business. We can text or email from HubSpot with ease, and it records all communication. With that said, we still set goals for outreach (outreach matrix), do the research, and make the calls daily. If it is worth doing, it is worth doing daily—no matter the size of the company.

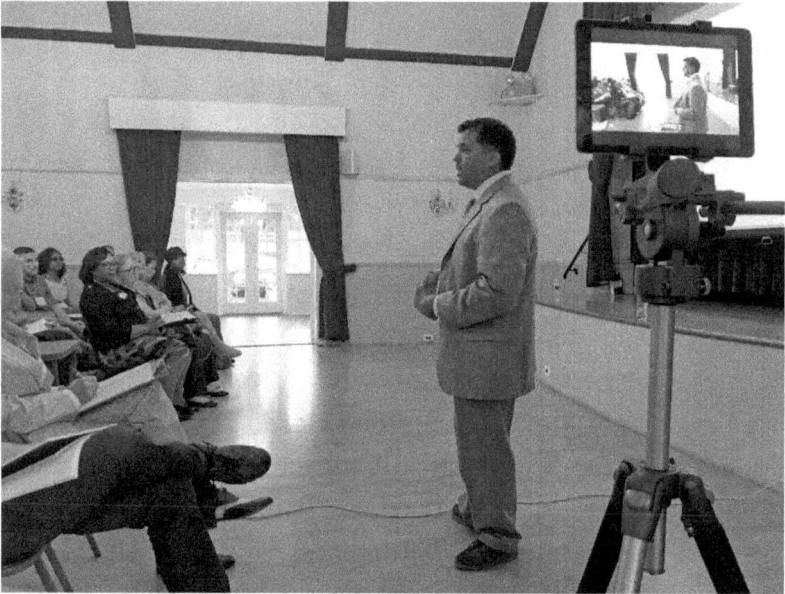

Speaking at Washington REIA in May 2017 - 1st Speaking
Engagement 1 month after first book comes out

Guest Speaker to Bay Area REIA Group in July 2019

Martin Saenz to the left. Shawn Muneio to the right

Ruth Saenz far left, Martin Saenz left, Shawn Muneio right,
Tiffany Muneio far right

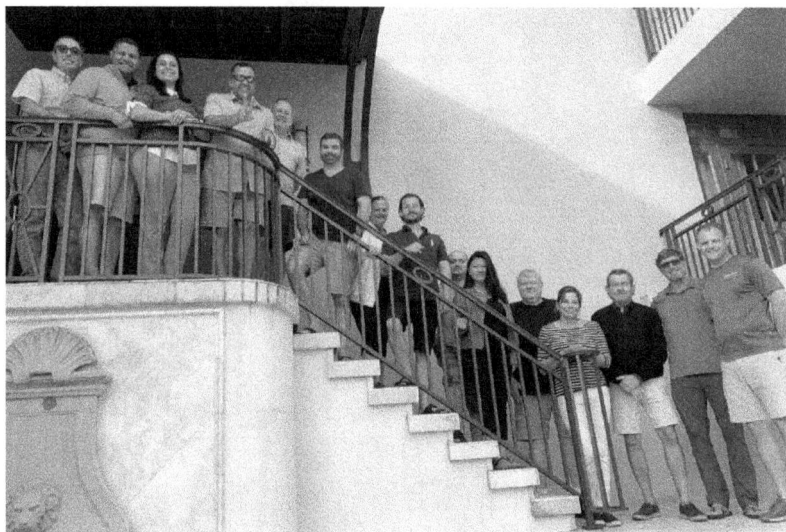

Note Investing Made Easier Mastermind Retreat in Destin, FL on October 2020

Martin and Ruth's four children

Stepping beyond Your Comfort Zone

Sometimes sourcing outreach may frustrate you. You may wonder whether the systems described above are right for you. Ultimately, you need to find systems that give you the freedom of time or whatever unique goals you are seeking. Talking to new people in hopes of building potential partnerships takes time and courage for most, but the rewards are there for those who persevere.

Flashback with me briefly.

When I was about ten years old, I was with my cousin in San Antonio for the summer. He was a teenager at the time. We took the bus downtown and spent the day walking around and watching a movie. Before we got on the bus to get home, he told me that he didn't have any more money for us to get home. We were stranded. The tone of the day shifted because we had to figure out some way to get home, and we were already getting tired.

"Hey, you need to start asking people for loose change," he told me.

Being a somewhat introverted kid, this was drastically out of my comfort zone. But I had to. The why was so big, the necessity of it all, that I didn't have a choice. I started asking a few people for money, and some of them gave it to me. After about fifteen minutes of this, my cousin started laughing at me.

"I have money. I was just joking with you," he admitted. I guess he thought that was funny. Regardless, that's an example of how when things get tough, you will step up to the plate and do what you have to do. You never know how strong you can be until you're in a position to exercise it.

I have confidence in you—the kind of confidence you may not have in yourself at this moment. We can push through that together. You're going to have to step outside of your comfort zone, and setting up the right systems can make it easier.

Systems, Systems, Systems

Sometimes the path of least resistance will get you the same result. Ideally, systems will make your life easier and put measurable controls around every facet of your business. They bring predictability to what you are looking to accomplish. At Bequest, we use several controls during each phase:

- **Sourcing phase.** We use a customized HubSpot that gives us marketing penetration data, pipeline management, email campaigns, prospect data, and investor information. We have goals in each area that are automatically measured, and we review results often.

- **Due diligence phase.** We have a team that assembles with each new trade. Each team member handles a specific due diligence task with and as established with our SOPs. Our controls include property valuation, skip tracing, credit report analysis, bankruptcy searches, title report reviews, and collateral reviews.

- **Asset management.** Our asset managers work on mortgage notes like an orchestra conductor. We have a set approval process to ensure legal evaluates each step before we order the service. During our borrower outreach process, all outreach is recorded for posterity and quality control. During our loan resolution process, each offer to borrowers is crafted through a consistent system, and timelines are monitored. Finally, our borrower relations management database is customized to capture and maintain key borrower data points.

- **Portfolio management.** We hold monthly budget review meetings where the CFO presents the budgeted and actual numbers. She is a thirty-year veteran in the banking industry and would make your mind blow up if you sat in on your first session. We look at metrics such as investment to value, collectability percentages, equity coverage, and actual vs. budget results.

Just like how you have a living financial statement to understand your financial health, you will need to build a living operation manual to track the systems you put into place. Some practices you will pick up from other players, and some you will self-develop, but maintaining a comprehensive living operations manual will maximize the predictability of your business investments.

As you work on your sourcing system, consider Paperstac. It is an online marketplace for buying and selling loans, and it streamlines the process of obtaining notes. If you're a new note buyer, it puts you in connection with veteran note sellers. From a sourcing perspective, this is invaluable. If you let it, it may even spoil you! It is also a great tool for seasoned note investors who are looking to streamline and optimize their own processes in this ever-evolving industry. You can leverage their systems and set up alerts when notes become available that fit your buying parameters. It is all fully digitized. I interviewed the founder of

Paperstac, Rick Allen, to give you a better idea of their process and give you more context to consider whether to incorporate Paperstac into your system of controls.

Interview with Rick Allen

Martin: Can you tell me about Paperstac and how my readers can use it?

Rick: We are a completely online marketplace for buying and selling loans. What we've done is take the process of buying a loan and streamline it by digitizing the process and creating a digital audit trail.

The great thing about Paperstac is that digital copies of the loans can be uploaded, so you can go through the process of looking at the collateral file, the assignments, and the allonges. An allonge is necessary when there is insufficient space on the document itself for endorsements. When it's time to fund a deal, it goes through a collateral audit by a third party. That way, you can verify what you have already seen as actually true.

The biggest thing we've seen is that it's an efficient tool for investors coming into the note space. We've had several first-time buyers who want to conduct business with sellers who've been in the business for years. We made it so someone who's new to note buying can come in there and buy a note and do everything digitally.

We're integrated with several vendors, and we provide the ability to purchase things like O&E reports and EPOs. We are integrated with a third-party collateral audit who will put their hands on the physical collateral and go through it and verify what is original and what's not—like liens, for example. That's why I say we help with the dotting of the Is and crossing of the Ts.

Martin: Do you think Paperstac's whole process of paper flow and due diligence can help newer investors become more proficient with buying notes?

Rick: Yes, 100 percent. One of our new features is ideal for new investors. They can go there and access the note-trading simulator. They can buy and sell a loan with fake money first and start practicing running their due diligence via the actual play of buying a loan.

Martin: What kind of advantages do you have in the marketplace? And please touch on Paperstac as a trade desk for larger hedge funds.

Rick: First, we view ourselves as the first, 100 percent digital note product. There have been several other marketplaces out there—and it's not my style to bash other marketplaces. They can be effective. We just feel that we've put a little extra technology into it and focused on automating the entire process, using technology to replace what a human would do.

As far as hedge funds, we are working with several large ones that are looking at Paperstac as a way to put their inventory out there and touch retail investors. This provides a conduit for a first-time buyer to get in there and purchase from a hedge fund that's been operating for a decade. They can do business together.

The hedge fund is utilizing Paperstac as a risk management tool because it provides a digital audit trail and also because of the efficiency it provides. It allows them to manage multiple assets with the click of a button. We have a lot of veteran buyers coming in here who have been around for years. We have institutional players who have been in the industry for twenty-five years conducting transactions. If nothing else, it's about the efficiency of everything.

When you're getting on Paperstac, you want to set up your search parameters. If you're only buying notes in a certain geolocation, say Florida, that is first position, under $175,000 in balance, and has a blue house, you want to set that and save that search. When that asset comes onto the platform, it sends you an alert that says, "Hello, you've got an asset that matches your buying criteria."

For the people who are still working that nine-to-five job and making a transition into notes full time, this allows them to be working on this while they're working on their day job. It's not just an extension for the big hedge funds in that regard. It's good for anyone getting into the business as a way to source good inventory.

And if you're going to make this into a business, you have to set up the infrastructure to move forward. If you buy a handful of loans at a time without the right infrastructure in place, it gets tricky. I love that you're teaching people how to do all this efficiently, and we can certainly help too.

> **Martin:** Traditionally, we think of sourcing as a one-way street—what you're doing to bring inventory to the table. You're making it so inventory can find you, the investor, and that's a unique proposition in terms of asset acquisition.
>
> **Rick:** It's all about leveraging your time. That is the one currency we all have the same amount of and can't get back once it's spent. You have to leverage your time, and Paperstac is a tool to make that process easier than ever. I highly encourage your readers, whether they are new to the note space or seasoned investors, to check out Paperstac and see what we can do for them.

As Rick shows, Paperstac is all about leveraging your time. Readers, feel free to check out Paperstac. You can sign up at https://pstac.co/jd3/ to get a discount.

The name of the game is deal flow. I keep pounding that point home because I'm just so emphatic about it. Deal flow is one of my chief passions in life, but knowing how to keep it going is a process. It's like playing a game where the rules are constantly changing.

My book came about because our industry is always evolving. If you don't evolve with it, you will grow stale, and stale companies, as Steve pointed out earlier, fail. We must evolve with the times, and that's what this is about.

I will be recommending Paperstac throughout the book, so I want you to continue to think and respond interactively. Otherwise, you will be spinning your wheels, wasting time and money, until you have the proper system of controls in place.

Always remember, deal flow is king, and it begins with a strong sourcing plan with controls to keep things predictable.

CHAPTER 6

◆ ◆ ◆

Balancing Capital and Partnerships

When I started note investing, I had $225,000 in capital buying first-mortgage notes. I had read some books, but mostly, I learned as I went along—and took a lot of hits because of it. If only I knew then what I know now. I could have saved tens of thousands of dollars and hundreds of hours of time. If you follow the advice in this book, *Note Investing Made Easier*, and *Cashflow Dojo*, you'll have a comprehensive look at the note industry that will help you avoid my mistakes. Together, they provide a complete equation for starting a note business.

At this point, though, you probably have some questions but may still feel ready to buy a note right now. That's the passion starting to take hold. Trust me, you will still benefit from building an action plan and setting up the right systems. With both of those in place, you will receive note opportunities on an ongoing basis and have plenty of opportunities to ramp things up and buy all the notes your heart desires.

If you start buying right out of the gate without having a model set up, however, your weaknesses will come at you in full force and work against you. We haven't even discussed investor capital yet! As I've tried to make clear, it is not enough to simply attend conferences or jump in and buy your first note. You need a plan and research. Get to know the industry players. Connect with them. Learn. Grow. Again, if it is worth doing, it is worth doing daily. Just think, everyone at a conference is distracted with their own agenda and network. Breaking in is difficult if you have not built a plan in advance. Deal flow will come if you diligently work on your foundation—the 3 Cs.

That foundation is key. You don't need an expensive degree. You don't even need much capital to be successful in the note industry, especially when you are starting out (though it certainly helps). If you move forward with a well-formed plan, you can build a business based on your diligence, passion, and commitment to strategic partnerships.

Passion

Passion and belief go hand in hand. If you have a lot of passion, and you know your "why," you don't need a lot of capital coming right out of the gate. I know this from personal experience. In fact, a host of very successful note investors started with very little capital. Oftentimes they enter this space, having been sleeping in their parent's basement and eating leftovers for days on end. You should hear their stories. I love to hear them. They come in flat broke and destitute, but you know what? They now have a successful note business, and it started with one key ingredient, passion.

My Journey with My Business Partner

I think back to how I met my business partner, Shawn Muneio. One month after publishing *Note Investing Made Easier* in 2017, Shawn reached out to me for mentorship. We spent the weekend together in DC, and I mentored him for six months. Shawn comes from the fintech world and has a lot of experience in finance and technology. As someone who still uses a financial calculator and whiteboard, I am light-years behind him in that regard. What stood out to me about Shawn was that he did everything I asked of him. If I handed him notes to evaluate, he would work until 3:00 a.m. to produce results. That's in addition to holding a corporate job and managing a family. He more than proved his loyalty, work ethic, values, and results. We started doing deals together and later formed a partnership in 2019. I credit much of our success to his attention to detail and ability to ensure everything we do is profitable. I am blessed to have him in my life. His strengths more than offset my weaknesses, and vice versa. This is what you should look for in a partner, should you decide you need one.

Mastermind Groups

Likewise, you will benefit from finding an action partner—or a few of them. You're going to connect with people you resonate with from a value perspective and from a buying parameter perspective, and those relationships can be invaluable. They're going to be sourcing deal flow, and you can work together to lock in trades. Working in a group, you can jump on a large opportunity together for a major boost to capital.

As you connect with action partners, strategic partners, and borrowers, just remember one thing—you have to vet everyone in this industry. Fortunately, you already have the tools to do this, such as skip tracing, for example. It's advantageous to vet people openly and have them vet you as well. You're putting a lot of trust in the people you come into contact with, and your livelihood is at stake. Their livelihood is at stake. This is serious. Be transparent. Do it openly. Say, "You can vet me too!"

You can then incorporate these key partners into a mastermind or some kind of strategic meetup. Find people with similar values and integrity in your niche and come together, in person or via video conferencing, once per month or once per quarter to discuss topics like sourcing, strategies, goals, asset management, schedules, and branding—those sorts of things. These sorts of conversations are incredibly effective and cost very little to no money to do.

The key is just to make sure that you're surrounding yourself with people who are going to elevate you! You can connect with one hundred people in a group, but only three of those individuals might have the reputation, collateral, or commitment to be worth working with. If you go in with a critical mind, it doesn't hurt to attend one of these strategy sessions. See how it goes, avoid making uninformed commitments, and identify those who might be worth knowing more about. Who knows, you may find note-investing rock stars you really gel with. Once you've done this with a few groups, you can bring your new winning contacts together into your mastermind group.

In a mastermind, each member can deliver some value to other members of the group. There are some existing mastermind groups in the note industry, but some do not operate in the true spirit of a mastermind and instead serve more as training programs. I recommend building a true mastermind for yourself to help your business grow.

The Right Partnerships Pay Off

What will you provide? What about them? When forming any sort of partnership, know that up front and clearly communicate roles and responsibilities. Once you have the right support and processes in place, you will be better able to buy notes at the right place and then work them out.

Maybe you're someone who has a little bit of capital already, but you feel like you may exhaust it in a fairly short amount of time. If that's your concern, know that most of what we have talked about thus far should not cost you much (if any) money. For now, put the topic of raising investor capital on the back burner. Instead, think about the relationships you need to build in the industry.

If you are just starting out, you should have a tab in your CRM system for investment capital partners, but definitely let them know you're not set up to receive any investment capital yet. You're just looking to see if there's any interest. Find people within the note space who have capital and who are connected on a good amount of deal flow—they will be your greatest resources going forward. In these early stages, ask yourself these questions to make sure you have a plan:

- What are my strengths, and who do I need to partner with to offset my weaknesses?
- What am I looking to accomplish with note investing?
- Do I need a coach or mentor to help keep me on track?
- Is there any reason I cannot put in the necessary work to make this happen?
- What will life look like if it does not happen?
- Who else needs to be on board with this endeavor?
- Do I need leverage? If so, how much?
- Do I need employees? If so, how many and for what roles?
- Do I need a joint-venture partner? If so, what will they bring to the table, and how do we structure it so that everyone wins?

If you are an established note investor, you can ask:

- Has my business scaled to the level I need it to?
- What do I need to remove from my business?
- What do I need to add to my business?
- Given the tools I'm learning in this book, what will I commit to doing differently going forward?

If you can answer those questions, you'll have a better idea of who you should be reaching out to. Know what kind of investor or individual you are looking for, then put a tab in your CRM for that. It all goes back to due diligence and systems.

Creativity Is a Must in Today's Market

Different partners have different interests. The name of the game is helping people get closer to their goals as you get closer to yours. Your job is to find out people's goals and find people whose goals match up with yours or what you do. When note prices were cheaper, you could talk to your Aunt Susie, have her cut you a check for $50,000, take that money to the marketplace, buy a few notes, and split the profits. Everybody wins, and everybody is happy.

In today's market, you need to be operating upstream—that is, in larger deals with bigger deal flow opportunities and more advantageous price points. You have to be creative, ahead of the curve, and maybe borrow money from other note investors.

When I wrote this book, I was involved in a $3 million opportunity. My partner and I had $1 million to work with, and we found a capital partner for the additional $2 million. That is the beauty of the industry: you can create your own opportunities, and the leverage always goes to the party that sources the deal. You have to be creative like that. Having the right strategic partnerships in place delivers results—plus, it's a win-win model. It's hard to go wrong when it's a win for you and a win for your partners. I source these types of deals with my group all of the time.

Source in pools.

Carve yourself into the action.

Don't be shy.

On a daily basis, you'll be making connections with sellers—people who work at trade desks for hedge funds or independent note sellers—and you are sourcing deals that benefit them. You can connect the seller with the buyer and put yourself into the action, whether you charge a consulting fee or get some notes out of the deal. The key is to do this daily.

Identify as a Good Partner

The investment opportunities will be there. You may need to be a licensed broker, as I said, for certain types of deals, but there are ample other opportunities in this space if you want to go another route. You just want to be diligent with your systems and stay in creation mode.

Being a manager is one route. You can manage notes as an *asset manager* for other note investors who buy fifty or one hundred notes and have a full-time job. They get tapped out with time, so they need someone to support them on the backend and manage their portfolio. As an asset manager, you can take those notes from nonperforming to performing. That's the idea.

There's ongoing maintenance to make sure the performing notes stay performing. At Bequest, our controller produces a daily delinquency report for the asset manager, whose sole job is to get in contact with borrowers to encourage them to stay on track with their payment schedule. This task is not overly complex, but daily commitment to this effort produces serious gains.

Doing something like asset management requires very little capital right out of the gate, if any capital at all, as long as it's set up correctly. If you're very good with details, this can be a way to carve out some space for yourself in the industry.

Alternatively, you could offer due diligence support. There's always a huge need for this, especially for major players who already have a lot of deal flow. You might help them by pulling credit reports or doing county record research. You can support just a few of these tasks, or you can run the full business for a buyer, allowing them to go into more trades. If you do that, your compensation might be a consulting fee or full notes. This can get you into the note space and earning notes with very little starting capital.

There are plenty more opportunities within the note space to create revenue—too many to list here adequately. When I talk about this with new or prospective note investors, the excitement begins to build, and they begin thinking of ways to jump right in and get started. I think that's great.

As you're reading this, you may be thinking of ways to get involved right now. Go ahead and write down your thoughts on how you see yourself operating in the note space. Free thinking is a lost art, so be the one to revive it. I just advise you to keep in mind what we've covered so far, from analyzing your strengths and weaknesses to setting up the proper systems.

You'll need to do your due diligence before jumping in, but in the coming chapters, we'll investigate in much more detail a few other ways you could get involved. Leveraging your resources and connecting with the right people will get you far in the note space.

In my early note-investing days, I didn't always practice the best due diligence, and let me tell you, the results reflected that. I will highlight one such occasion briefly in the next chapter, but I want to help you avoid the headache of lost time and money that I faced. In the following chapter, we'll look at the concept of due diligence, specifically in terms of putting the right systems in place for you as you look at the various industries within this space.

CHAPTER 7

◆ ◆ ◆

Due Diligence Controls

In my first book, *Note Investing Made Easier*, I covered what I called the three-round due diligence process. The first round involved evaluating the underlying collateral on the asset—the property. In this stage, I look at data that helps me determine the value of the property as an investment, including fair market value, back taxes, ownership information (e.g., if it's owner occupied), neighborhood, nearby schools, and so on. The second round of due diligence deals with evaluating the borrower and their ability to pay you, as well as further analysis of the property. The third round involves reviewing the data and projecting the ROI of the investment.

Due diligence comes down to you having the correct systems in place when you have deal flow coming in; it's a funneling process. Let's say you want to work a large deal on your own. You need to understand each step, price each note accordingly, and then cherry-pick which notes you want to buy. The funneling process is a matter of prioritizing essentially, or phasing out those notes that don't meet your parameters while keeping the ones that do. You will be able to assign value to a particular note and decide whether you want to keep it before putting in offers.

A great way to do this is to use a matrix, which we'll discuss at the end of this chapter. First, we'll talk more about the various rounds of due diligence, so you have a foundation on which to craft a strong pricing matrix. From there, you can create a due diligence action plan to put your systems together.

As covered in *Note Investing Made Easier*, we employ a three-round due diligence process that we have refined over the years. Round one deals with the property, round two involves both the property and the borrower, and round three rolls it up from a financial return perspective.

Due Diligence Round One

I usually start with RealtyTrac. It can give you the fair market value of a note, with sales comps to back up that value. Those sales comps have a lot to do with the property description and recent sales of nearby properties that closely match your property description. You can also gain useful ownership information with RealtyTrac during this first pass, specifically information on who the property is registered to. Regardless of which vendor you use for property details, you want to triangulate the data with the many online sites out there to ensure the quality of the data.

You will need to match all this information with the information given to you on the tape you received. If RealtyTrac has different information than reported by the seller, then the property may have gone through a foreclosure process and ownership change, meaning you're no longer looking at a note with a valid lien. You will want to avoid those types of notes.

You will also look at transaction information and note any history of foreclosure, ownership changes due to divorces or other factors, the most recent property purchase date, and any other transaction information. You can also note which companies have liens on the property, which can be helpful.

During this round, you will also want to do a county record search. This includes looking at county sites, gathering back tax information, and seeing where the tax bills are getting mailed to. You might also find out whether the property is owner occupied, which is important. If you're someone like me who's looking to let homeowners stay in their homes, then knowing whether the homeowner uses the property as their primary residence is important.

If you're buying a first mortgage, you're probably going to pull an owner's and encumbrances report, but we pull them when we purchase junior lien mortgages too. This document is like a title source and will list all the liens on the property, the amounts of those liens, HOA status, encumbrances, the owner of the property, and the chain of assignments of lien holders. All of that is important for due diligence.

The Broker Price Opinion

During this stage, you'll want to get a broker's price opinion (BPO). With this, a real estate agent or a broker will take some pictures of the outside and consider the property description and the sales comps to assign it an estimated fair market value.

You don't want to discount the value that a realtor brings to the table. When I got into the note space in 2013, I was buying notes in the Ohio area and spent about ten days doing the drive-bys myself. This cut into the time I could have spent doing other kinds of due diligence, which cost me. In one instance, a house that I believed had a fair market value of about $85,000 ended up only being worth $25,000. During my drive-by, I had missed that the property was only a block or so away from a distressed neighborhood—boards on the windows and doors, spray paint. It was a run-down area.

Don't make that same mistake. Never discount the value of a good realtor who knows the area. Instead of doing drive-bys, deepen other aspects of your due diligence.

Second Mortgages Are Significantly More Involved

With small-balance junior liens, we normally will pull a property report to get information on property liens without doing a full-blown title search. The property report typically provides a comprehensive view of the property information, including characteristics, location, zoning, flood information, owner vesting, last two market sales, mortgage recording information, and basic tax information, including assessed value and current-year property tax information. Even if you are buying performing notes, information like this can be invaluable.

Due Diligence Round Two

Round two of due diligence deals with the borrower and their ability to pay. If you're only looking at first-mortgage notes, you really won't need to worry about skip tracing because you know that you're, in all likelihood, going to get the property back if you run into a borrower issue. In that case, you might be able to do just round one of due diligence. However, I always try to understand the borrower and their ability to pay based on an analysis of their credit report and other reports I research.

Due Diligence Round Three

Everything that I do goes back to that and keeping in line with who it is that's putting money in my pocket. In this case, it would be the borrower, the homeowner. I roll up the results into a cash-on-cash spreadsheet that helps me determine the price I need to pay in order to achieve the return I need to achieve. This is due diligence round three: evaluating all the information you've gathered.

The Right Vendor Partners

When planning your due diligence process, you need to know your vendors. You shouldn't just go out and buy a note that seems appealing; you need to collect data from vendors to inform you of your approach. Here are a few for you to consider.

Initially, I relied on Richmond Monroe and a creditor rights attorney to review collateral documents. At Bequest, we use Credco as our credit-pulling service. Analyzing credit reports and other data sources will give you a fuller picture of the type of borrower you are dealing with, thereby informing your investment.

I use Lexis Nexus for skip tracing, but Tracers is another go-to option for many. Both give you information about a person's occupation and overall character. Since you are buying mortgages on the secondary mortgage market, you do not get the luxury of interviewing the homeowner prior to purchasing their mortgage.

You'll also need to get set up at https://pacer.gov/ to do bankruptcy searches. If they have filed for bankruptcy, you can get a wealth of information from this website. You also will want to receive a legal review of the bankruptcy case if you are on the newer side of investing.

I recommend RealtyTrac for searching fair market value, liens, sales comps, and ownership information. This tool will provide information on real estate trends, property values, individual property sale history, ownership information, and much more.

Knowing Your Process

There are so many routes you can take when note investing, but due diligence is key to all of them. You need to nail down your process for the route you wish to go. For instance, I can't speak on contracts for deeds (CFDs). It's a lot of seller finance paper and land contracts. It's not my area of expertise. In my opinion, CFDs are associated with low-dollar properties and lower outstanding principal balances. All in all, I believe there is too much risk involved with these types of notes, but that could be due to my limitations as an investor. There is a lot of inventory out there, but the easiest path is not always the best path. If it does not fit in with my business model or jive with my mission statement, it is a hard pass for me. That sort of discernment will serve you well.

Once you get yourself set up and buy a few notes for yourself, nail down the due diligence process. However, I advise starting slow. You can revise your systems and processes as you move along. When you do buy, you may want to take advantage of notes with low unpaid principal balances. Many note investors do not want those, but you might decide that you want to go that route, especially if sourcing is a problem for you. You're going to have to go through the same due diligence process with those, and the same legal effort, as with anything else, but your capital outlay is reduced.

You will likely find, however, that the reward is not worth the time investment. If you want to just simulate these sorts of deals or other types of deal flow, you can go back to Paperstac. Its simulation feature allows you to go through the process of doing your due diligence with fake money. It's a great way to increase your experience and comfort before officially entering the marketplace and placing yourself at risk.

PRICING MATRIX		
	1ST IS PERFORMING	**1ST IS NON-PERFORMING**
FULL EQUITY	50 CENTS	30 CENTS
PARTIAL EQUITY	40 CENTS	20 CENTS
NO EQUITY	20 CENTS	3 CENTS
*PRICING IS AN ARBITRARY NUMBER USED FOR DEMONSTRATION PURPOSES ONLY		

Build a Pricing Matrix to Systemize Your Buying

If you're buying junior liens, you're going to spend a lot of time with RealtyTrac, credit reporting, skip tracing efforts, first-mortgage performance data, and county reports. With this information, you can create a pricing matrix.

You can build a rough draft of a pricing model right now. Below is a sample of one you can create in Excel, but you can make yours more sophisticated if it helps your process.

In this simple matrix, we have four different grades with four different boxes. The credit report and title report should give you guidance on the performance of the senior mortgage, and RealtyTrac and BPOs should help you understand the equity coverage for the note.

One of the boxes, for example, deals with performing notes. As you grade the notes and understand which ones fall into which category, you'll have your pricing done in advance. Again, all of these are things you can do before a deal ever comes down the pipeline.

Your process will look something like this—you perform due diligence on each note based on the already established matrix categories, then you're going to assign pricing for those notes, and then roll that pricing up and make your offer.

Due Diligence Is a Team Sport

You need to involve vendors, partners, realtors, and attorneys when performing due diligence, especially in the beginning. When you get your business to a certain volume, you will be able to replace these parties with employees who are committed and work together in a physical corporate environment. At Bequest, for example, we have a director of asset management, collateral manager, controller, and several analysts who help with each note trade. Shawn runs that department with much care.

You may want to consider recruiting some good trade partners or becoming part of a buyer's group to hone your due diligence process. Getting good results often depends on the success of your peer outreach and your peer sourcing. Put that to work for you. Every week, you should be reaching out to your peers, developing relationships, and finding partners. Find people who can bring expertise to the vetting process. Let's say you broker a deal with twelve notes. You call a seasoned note player and ask them to partner on the deal, giving them five notes if they help you oversee the due diligence process. They might be able to give you a crash course in how they do their due diligence.

Just be creative!

I highly encourage you to be cautious of groups that pressure you to buy notes without giving you time to conduct due diligence. If the environment is not in line with your value systems and triggers your internal alarm, you should respectfully move on. That group is not going to help you grow and be autonomous as a highly successful note investor in your own right. You will find the right groups that resonate with you—or you can form one yourself.

Likewise, let's say someone wants to bring me into a group they control so they can sell me on a certain deal flow, which they also control. This is a code red signal to get out of that group as quickly as possible. If you're in a group where someone else is always calling the shots, you can become a good helper, but it will also keep you in that student mindset we're trying to avoid—and it will be hard to develop your own autonomy and grow.

Embrace the giver's gain mentality when seeking due diligence partners. I believe that the value I put into a group should be at least equal, if not greater, to the value that I get in return. That approach has led to many of my long-standing relationships in this space.

There is value in teamwork and the relationships we build. I've been exposed to some groups that are very tight with structure and quality players, but no one is actively sourcing for the group. If you form a group, sourcing has to be at the forefront of the group's focus, and do not discount making performance-based reward systems to drive deal flow.

Surround yourself with people who have a good reputation and integrity. As you talk to people, you'll hear things like, "Stay away from so and so because they've screwed over a bunch of investors." On the other hand, you might find someone who just seems to be a magnet for deal flow.

Finally, keep your niche in mind. In the note investor space, I'm considered a junior lien player, but I have first-mortgage and business notes too, and I consider myself a cash flow guy even though I may be lumped into a certain category. I buy junior liens because I find them at better price points. Their fair market values are much higher than first-mortgage notes. You can build a sustainable note business for yourself. You may be able to find some peers who will sell you their notes, or you might find some notes from investors who have notes that are outside of their typical buying parameters. They may not have time to work on them, and you can get some notes that way. But at the end of the day, you really don't have strong controls when you're just relying on external factors or being at the right place at the right time to receive some notes here and there.

The key is to build internal systems that support your niche. You want to build a business model to ensure you have that constant deal flow coming in. If you don't have that right now, then you have a lot of work to do right now. Look at your buying parameters, and see what you prefer to buy so that when a buying opportunity becomes available, you'll be ready with the strategic partners or team members you need and are aligned with— including on price. You do not want to be in a situation where you're force-fed what the pricing should be; that could lead to complications. Be the one bringing deals to the right table, and others will love you for it. This is the whole point of the control phase: having control over sourcing and due diligence as well as asset management on the backend. By forging relationships, you are ready for massive takedowns.

CHAPTER 8

◆ ◆ ◆

Asset Management Is
Project Management

At Bequest, we have SOPs that ensure the continued performance of the mortgages in our income fund. Our project management involves the coordination and organization of various activities aimed at maximizing the recovery of outstanding debts while maintaining a high level of efficiency and compliance. How well you project manage the systems you build, and how well you tie together all of the various pieces to access information as circumstances arise, directly correlates to how successful you can be in this space.

Project management will help you simplify things—to slow down all of the moving parts around you. It's another control you can put on each phase of note investing (sourcing, due diligence, asset management, and portfolio management), increasing the efficiency and predictability of your business.

A note investor is like an orchestra conductor. They stand before an array of musicians with all of the different instruments, and they direct each piece succinctly in order to produce a specific result that is uniform. The different instruments are tantamount to the various activities you will be managing at any given point. It's your job to manage all of these activities efficiently to produce a good deal flow. You are on a stage, and the peers that you source are your audience.

I often think back to when I first started note investing. The space has changed rapidly since then. I used an Excel spreadsheet for project management. My other tools were a folder system and a borrower relations management template with which I could capture pertinent borrower information and ongoing activity or correspondence information. Admittedly, it was pretty simple, but for the most part, it worked well for me.

Project management can be done in a variety of ways, and my former protégé and colleague, Alira Morstadt, of AMSquared Investment Group has her own great system, which she now licenses as a custom-built PODIO system. (I was one of her first paid subscribers.) Below is an interview where she talks about her system, and it might give you some ideas that might help you as you're coming out of the gate.

Interview with Alira Morstadt

Martin: Alira, can you explain what works for you?

Alira: Physically, I have a collateral file for each file. While they are in the pipeline, which is the process between nonperforming notes and performing, I have a set of drawers.

If I have time to enter or record, I see who I can contact, and I have a visual representation of where those files are. So it's a very intentional movement for me.

I want those files to move from the bottom shelf, which is when I first get them, on through the stages until they are performing. Then I can file them away in my filing cabinet. It's a visual thing for me, and it's very intentional.

I focus in the morning to try and get those files moving upward (to where they are performing) because that's moving through the pipeline. Then, to track that where I can easily see an overview of how my files are set up, I have a whiteboard that tracks exactly where they are in the pipeline; that's where I keep my active notes once they become performing. Unless I'm notified otherwise, they're not my initial focus.

I've done borrower outreach on these ten files, for instance, and let's say I haven't heard from them. I can move them to a follow-up, and then if I continue to not hear from them, I can go through the proper legal channels. I can prepare for legal at that point, send files off to legal, or see where they are.

Everything for me is visual.

Now, let's discuss how I arrived at this system.

Firstly, I got a filer at IKEA that was large enough for my legal files. I can put two in one drawer.

Second, because my husband and I work together, he needs to see and know exactly where things are in the pipeline by simply looking at the board and then finding them in the files.

Martin: Alira has set up a good system that uses strong visual aids to track the flow of her note workouts. Some people work better this way, and she couples this tracking system with a custom-built data management system, as we'll discuss. Now, Alira what are some of your other day-to-day activities?

Alira: In terms of my regular day-to-day, I think you covered the importance of developing and maintaining a daily ritual. That was a big part of my training as well. That's always been very important to you as I can attest. I'll tell you some of the things I put on my whiteboard each day.

Especially when a *new* deal comes in, it's really important that I have complete collateral.

For example, I am still awaiting three assignments of mortgages (AOMs) on the last trade we did, and those that need to be reformatted, so I've got them awaiting cures.

In terms of channels, if the borrower outreach channel isn't successful, then I can filter that back to the legal one. I have notes pending payoffs that are pending workouts, pending sales too. There are a lot of different things that I have checks for.

Let's say I have a note that's pending sale, for example. I need to make sure that I'm keeping track of it because they might not be contacting me since I just had it recorded.

I send emails off to make sure that the seller knows that there should be a payoff coming in, and I need to get notified of that. That's important for me to know how to stay on top of that loan. I need to keep tracking that note and making sure that I'm on top of all that.

I also record my own AOMs too, or as many of them as I can. Sometimes the recording can take a week, two weeks, or two months, depending on the county, so I want that in a separate area altogether.

I use Simplifile too. When I'm waiting for something in the mail, for example, and when there's a good indication that things are awaiting the next action step, I need to look out for it further.

So I entered it into the software system that I created. That's where I keep track of everything, and that's where due diligence begins.

I do a completely renewed due diligence when I'm entering the notes in my computer system, and that's what my system is designed for—to make sure that there is no stone left unturned. I know everything about that note. I know everything that I need to know to hopefully achieve a successful outcome for myself, as well as the borrowers.

That's really important, and dependent on the requirements of that state of where the property is, I would either prepare them for legal, or I would prepare a welcome package to send out.

Martin: You also use software for project management. Tell me about when you were first introduced to PODIO and what your impressions of that were.

Alira: I had a bit of a misconception about PODIO. It was in my ear all the time about needing a CRM, and I guess I'm pretty basic with computers for the most part. I don't want to be managing a CRM all of the time. I have my phone. I want to keep it simple.

Then I saw some examples of what PODIO could do through a Facebook page and how it could be put to use and make everything more effective, more efficient. That is something that really drives me. I was using Excel and e-folders, which were doing the job but were not as efficient.

If I was given information on one borrower, and I needed to go to another borrower, I had to go *up* three levels and then *down* four on another one. You have to click twenty times to get to where you want to go, and that isn't always the most efficient system. When I saw the opportunity in PODIO, I still didn't recognize how great it was until I started playing around with it.

I also made a lot of modifications to my PODIO. I try to track as efficiently as possible. So when I get a collateral file, I have answers to questions like, What's the first thing I do? What's the first thing I look at? What information do I need?

I keep track of the information that I'm working with thanks to PODIO. If I'm 30 percent done on one note, 70 percent done on another note, or 100 percent done on yet another note, I can look at onboarding and see that straight away. I can see where I'm at on each note in particular. I can see what I need to keep focused on, then using the assets application, in one minute, I can take a look and see everything that I need to be doing to a note.

Sometimes, attorneys call me. I have to track that. I had a borrower call me out of the blue the other day as well. Within thirty seconds, I had all of the information up just like I would if I were a bank or a lender. You would expect them to verify who you are and have that information available, so that aspect of PODIO really helps.

If attorneys are calling, or you're calling them, you want that information to be right there. Just think about the financial impact of that. My attorneys remind me, "I'm charging you $287 per hour," so you want that information readily available. Especially in a state like Ohio where it's becoming litigious, I want to dot all my Is and cross my Ts.

Every bit of correspondence from speaking or emailing with a borrower, I have tracked. If it comes to the day when I have to appear in court, I can print off my notes, and I have that as validation of what has happened and/or been discussed.

As you know, we often deal with a lot of money, and there may be circumstances when you need to verify something, so you have to know what you said. Have it written down, and a time stamp is helpful too. With my system, you have that ability.

Martin: Based on the way you have customized PODIO for your own use, what are a couple of the most significant things that it does for you?

Alira: Tracking expenses is a big deal for me. I somewhat had my expenses tracked before, don't get me wrong, but it wasn't a very good system for me at all. Being able to pull up a ledger and see what the outcome was for a note helps you in many different ways. For one, it helps you with your ROI. Also, if a borrower comes to you with a payoff, you can look at that really quickly and see whether it's feasible. I use the expenses app every day, all day long. I track every single expense.

Additionally, you will be better able to understand which states you want to get into and which states you're going to want to avoid. It's good for tracking and recording and having everything at your fingertips. Within my PODIO application, I have access to e-files, credit reports, and everything to do with that file at the click of the mouse. Because it is there, I'm sitting at my desk with my computer open and PODIO running at all times.

I'm tracking information that would've been lost, and that's the biggest deal for me. Even though I was pretty good with my filing—I had an efficient or workable system—there was a lot of information being lost. I would have to stop and look up the numbers to make phone calls. Now, I have the CRM within PODIO, and I can look up and find out all of the information I can about one county.

The chief concern for me, with this PODIO application, was easily accessing everything, having everything in one place, and only entering information once.

I have all the information I need about the city of Alexandria, for example. In PODIO, I can link that to any note. As soon as I get a note, and I see it is the city of Alexandria, I can pull up that county and see I'm not going to be able to do a title search because it's $500 per year. I stored all the information about that county in that place. Also, I can put in tips that I might need later.

Simply put, it's helping me organize all kinds of information. I feel that based on the increased organization provided, it helps me to optimize my note management far better. I particularly appreciate the next-step feature in my own system. I use the next-step feature every day. Before I exit from a note, for example, my next step is to confirm with the attorney and then double-check how I've got that set up.

I also feel that all these tools give me added credibility and profitability. I have no doubt. I'm entering all my own data. I know some people use virtual assistants, but I'm doing that myself, which helps me learn my notes better. Just the other day while in the car, a borrower called.

I was able to recall the information that I needed to verify quickly. I could address that call and build a relationship, and so that call was successful because I had learned the information. I highly recommend your readers use PODIO. It prevents things from falling through the cracks, as can happen sometimes even with one note. There are little things you should be tracking all the time, and this system allows you to track all of that. If I had this system when I started, I can't imagine how much more info I would have stored by now.

Between whiteboard, PODIO, and my other systems, all my basics are covered.

But to be fair, a gentleman named Richard McGrew built the foundation for my PODIO system, but he said that I had ended up changing his system so much that it was no longer the same. People can design their PODIOs to fit them. I have modified mine to fit how I do things, but it is still quite generic for the seconds market, and it's something that I think people could find really valuable.

Alira provides great insight into the value of putting the right systems in place—and homing in on the project management side of things—in order to achieve your overarching goals more efficiently.

If you're converting assets from nonperforming to performing, there's a lot of information you will be acquiring and storing for later. You have to be able to track all of that efficiently, just as a larger lending institution needs to do. It gives you credibility in that regard.

A good sound project management system will lead to better deal flow—*and* better cash flow. That last piece is our focus in the following chapter.

Part 3: Cash Flow Phase

CHAPTER 9

◆ ◆ ◆

Cash Flow Is Your Report Card

3 C's of Business

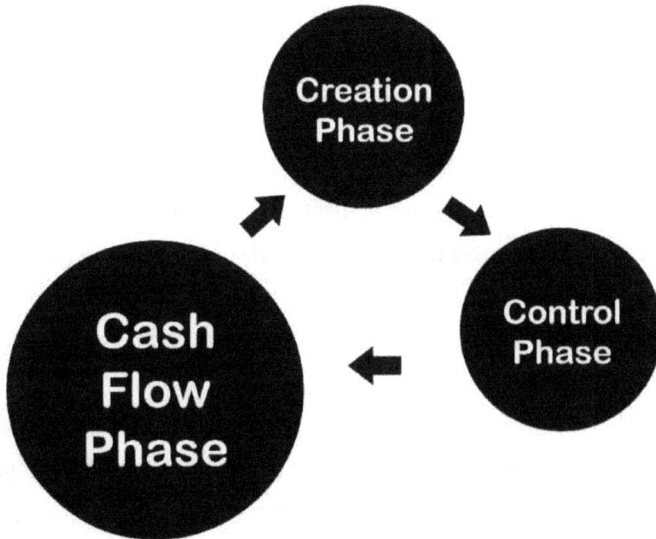

We've covered much so far, starting with building your road map and maintaining a living financial statement. We discussed the creation phase and the idea that you should always be in creation mode. That led us to focus on you finding your own business model. We discussed the various forms of mentorship and how those might be good ways for you to come out of the gate. From there, we looked at the control phase, beginning with how it relates to note sourcing. Those controls will lead to better deal flow, which is king—not cash. We talked about building your due diligence systems and explored the basics of project management with the help of Alira Morstadt.

All of this is part of the first two Cs: creation and control. If you do these first two Cs well, cash flow will be your reward. The cash flow phase is all about converting a distressed asset into a profitable asset and keeping the performing notes performing.

Build Your Business at Your Own Pace

While all of this may seem like a lot to absorb, just keep in mind—you can take it slow at first. Stick your toe in the shallow end. Don't run out and quit your day job tomorrow! Be mindful. If you are diligent and do each step properly, it will inevitably lead to deal flow. Better deal flow will lead to better cash flow, and that is the core of this business.

The best part is, you can form this note business for yourself while working your day job. Of course, once you start seeing traction in the note business, you'll be eager to quit. Good actions over time will pay off, but it is something that you can balance with your day job for now.

Maybe you came to this book as a result of watching some webinars, going to some social media outlets, or perhaps reading some other books. There are so many nuances to note investing that it may leave you in a state of confusion. For now, at the beginning of your journey, focus on your "why" and the fact that you *can* do this. With this one resource alone, you can start putting together that MAP and enacting the 3 Cs of your business. Starting slow does not mean that you are void of passion or commitment. In fact, if you're going to do this, starting slow will help make sure you adopt a growth mindset. As your business grows, you can refine your process and get tighter with your controls. By moving forward with a 360-degree process, cycling through the 3 Cs as you tamp down your burgeoning business, you'll find new and creative ways to improve what you do, create cash flow, and bolster your systems. It's an ongoing process.

Starting slow puts you in a mindset of scalability. Once you're doing well with ten notes or twenty notes, you can move to, say, a hundred notes, then two hundred, if you're comfortable with the leap, have strong systems in place, and remain committed to tweaking your controls. As you grow, you will see a parallel rise in your reputation and identity in the marketplace. If you're experiencing growth through the use of strategic partners, then your reputation and identity will grow even faster. Identities and reputations spread like wildfire. I have experienced it for myself and seen it with my colleagues.

If you're bringing in new deals and working with strategic partners who are also bringing you in on deals, people will see you as a professional. And, of course, you will be doing great from a cash flow standpoint. You are really on your game—and people will really start noticing—and that will lead to increased cash flow.

Time Really Is Money

In this industry, you get rewarded based on the level of effort you put in if you're doing things the right way. If you're doing well financially, and you're reputable, then in most cases, the note space is going to reward you. However, the more notoriety you get, the more you'll attract "time bandits." These are people who think they'll gain value from connecting with you. They will come in with the unexpressed goal of simply draining your resources.

We talked about the power of strategic partnerships and how important it is to choose wisely who you surround yourself with. You're doing this to build freedom of time. Time bandits would sap your freedom of time. You cannot allow people to take, take, take, without giving back. That would move you away from your "why" for note investing. At the end of the day, you want to work steadily toward your goals and only help others who'll help you get there.

Even though you may start doing well, your first investing model might not be your last. The note industry is constantly changing, and there are several industries within the broader industry itself. You need to stay flexible and watch what other people are doing with their models. You may want to try some of the things that they are doing. Take Alira, for example. Her project management is down pat, and that may be something that you decide to do for yourself.

I wish I could go back and obtain leverage partnerships and accountability partners much sooner. That would have absolutely propelled me further than I am right now. Once I discovered a passion for mentorship, though, I was instantly hooked. It excites me when I see the fruits of my labor—when protégés start gaining steam and have success of their own in the note business. They become colleagues, and if I can cut their learning curve and potential loss of time by a couple of years, then I consider that a success. I consider myself a mentor to my employees and investor partners now with Bequest Funds.

As you consider the trajectory of your business, I want to introduce you to Chaim Ekstein. He has some great investment strategies for the new note investor—and for the note investor trying to recapture deal flow. He is a brilliant man—a man of action who seems to stay one step ahead of most people. That's probably why we get along so great.

Chaim explains the cost of lost opportunities. As I demonstrated beforehand, sometimes you will try and fail, but I think you'll find that it's always better to try and fail than to never try at all. Not to mention, there are literally forty million reasons to consider the note space, as Chaim explains.

Interview with Chaim Ekstein

Chaim: You and I had a conversation before about how most people approach their financial planning. For most people, it goes something like this—they get an interesting idea from somewhere. If it makes sense, they engage in it, and they do as much research as they can. They consult with some professionals. Does it make sense or not make sense? They get other ideas. They are compiling stuff, which ends up in one big junk drawer with all kinds of stuff in it, and they're left not knowing whether and how one thing works with the other. They don't even know whether it works at all.

What successful people do, on the other hand, is that they take out the entire model. They approach it differently. They take those same ideas as the unsuccessful investor, but they begin to match those things up with the things that they are already doing. This is an important distinction. They are constantly matching new ideas to a deliberate, desired outcome.

Will this new idea help me with the other investments I have made? Will it help me with my retirement? Will it help me with my income taxes? Will it help me with my other taxes?

You have to know the effects on your tax liability. Will it help me with the other goals that I have? And so, as you can see, they start to make these sorts of connections for themselves.

If it makes sense, then they put it into play. If it doesn't make sense, they don't put it into play. Everything is working in harmony for the ultimate benefit of the overriding goals.

Martin: You have helped hundreds, if not thousands of people, in your career with their finances for a long period of time. How long have you been in business?

Chaim: I've been in business for over twenty years, going back to 1998, and I've seen a lot of things happening and a lot of situations during that time.

Martin: What do think the typical person coming into note investing may not be aware of?

Chaim: Note investing is not any different than it was when I started. Not really. It's the same thing. Most people look at note investing and wonder, does it make sense, does it not make sense, and that sort of thing. They decide at that point. They may not look at the big picture and discuss how their note investing will help them with their entire picture.

For instance, I had a conversation with a new note investor only recently, and I can give you some examples from that if you want, but I can't think of *any* money decision that wouldn't be better looking at its macro versus micro.

Martin: That's a great concept. Let's pursue that more. In terms of looking at the macro view of note investing from the perspective of a new note investor, he or she should look at their entire financial situation, build a financial statement, and look at the income they already have coming into the household versus all of the expenses going out, and assets and liability.

As they start to build a note business for themselves, they should consider products like life insurance products that could help them maximize the building of their new note portfolio.

Can you explain that a bit more?

Chaim: If you look at some insurance products, you can design them in a way where they are *designated* to enlighten the entire picture, like having certain insurance holdings as a holding tank. You store money there. From that portfolio, you fund your other investments. Then once you have positive cash flow, go back to the insurance strategy. It can accumulate and begin to fund more investments. When you look at it this way, *if* you have the proper guidance and the right person guiding you, you can not only succeed in note investing, but you can also gain a lot of benefits.

Of course, you can have benefits for your family. You can have planning that's going to help you with everything, but if you do it in the right way, you can end up being able to spend your death benefit while alive. Most people look at this as a death product. They think you have to die to get something, but you can ultimately end up spending that death benefit with certain strategies while you're alive just because you do it in a macro strategy.

I will give you an analogy. If you play chess, imagine how hard it would be to play without a board! It would be no fun at all. The same goes for financial planning. When people do the microplanning, it's like playing chess without a board. They don't have a model or anything to play against. They can't look out over the board and see the full picture.

When most people decide on life insurance, it's simple. "I want to protect my family," they say. They know how much they want to protect them. They know why they want to protect them. They're looking at life insurance strategies that make sense given their situation and unique circumstances.

They never look at how life insurance strategy can actually help them with their *entire* portfolio. It's oriented toward protection, and it will help build their assets. If you look at some insurance products, you can design them in a way that is designated to enlighten your entire financial portfolio. The key question is to ask yourself how can something that is oriented toward protection help me with my entire portfolio?

Martin: Most people think note investing has little to no tax advantage, and that's why you need real estate to offset it. But you're saying that it's just because a lot of people don't have it set up correctly. They don't have a supplemental vehicle or a parallel vehicle in the form of an insurance product from a professional that can feed into the note portfolio that then feeds back into the life insurance product.

Chaim: In my experience, most people don't take full advantage of what the government is telling them that they can take advantage of in terms of tax benefits. The number one reason is because of micro versus macro planning, but you have to start opening your eyes and open your mind. Your readers, for example, will want to begin associating with people who understand this stuff and then start looking at the macro picture with everything they're doing; it's amazing to see how much a person can accomplish with tax planning.

Most people look at it like this: I made $100,000. I had to pay my fair share of taxes. I'm left with about $66,700 for easy math, which seems pretty nice, but I'm going to look at the real cost of that $33,300 if you look at it in the macro picture. Let's put this $33,300 into my time value of money calculator. What would it have been worth in this hypothetical situation?

You also have to keep in mind, when you send in that money, at least in my case, they practically never send it back. You send it in and bye-bye. It's gone. So when you send something to someone like that, it's not only the cost, but there's also an opportunity cost—what could have been if I hadn't had to pay that.

If you're smart enough to realize that you're saving money by not sending that money to the government, then you're also smart enough to realize that you could possibly be receiving what you would have with note investing. Now the fun starts. We put a value of $33,300 into the payment field.

For a person thinking he could receive a 20 percent ROI on his investment, which comes to a future value of $39,356,656.25.

The cost of giving that money to the federal and state governments versus investing it is almost $40 million. If we look at it like that, we realize just how important it is to do something about that instead of sitting back and being passive. If you're not going to send that money to the government, you may as well invest it.

Martin: That's a lot of money, Chaim. What advice would you give my readers as they start learning how to save that money? Should they just go to E-Trade online or something like that? Is there some solution they can put this money into?

Chaim: If they don't want to pay $33,300 to the government, they have to start with some serious self-reflection. This is a critical step. They should feel the pain. They should want to do something about it.

If you want to get typical results, go the typical route. If you want to get the results that most people are getting, do whatever most people are doing. But what I'm talking about are out-of-the-box strategies. Merrill Lynch isn't interested in you knowing them. They want you to park your money. Say bye-bye. They want you to keep your money with them for as long as possible and never ask for anything in return, so you have to start being curious. Consult the very people who are doing these out-of-the-box strategies. Ask some questions. What are you doing? Can you help me get that done? I mean, it is very important. I want your readers to understand—it's their life at stake.

I advise you to be the captain of your own ship. Don't just believe people. Seek that advice out, but see it with your own eyes. Test it. Look at the macro picture. An airplane pilot, for instance, needs to know everything about the plane. He needs to know what might go wrong. They must understand everything, and it's the same way with your readers' finances. They must captain their own ships. Nobody cares about your own money more than you do.

So take charge. That doesn't mean that you will be an expert on everything, but you should be curious enough and interested enough to understand what is going on in your picture because it's not a $33,000 issue. When your accountant tells you that you're paying $33,000 on your passive income, it's not $33,000. It's $40 million.

You have forty million reasons to become inquisitive, find answers, get with the right people, and make your money work for you.

Martin: This is all about control and how you need to take ownership of your financial future and not leave it to fancy Wall Street salespeople. If you have some involvement in the assets you invest in, you can create a more predictable outcome. When should someone start getting their financial house in order? Is it before you start investing, or should you just be focused on earning income, and then those strategies will come into play later?

Chaim: The time is before. When you start to understand this type of stuff, this by itself will help motivate you and make you want to go out there. We looked at a thirty-year time frame, for example. Let's say it was only twenty-nine years, so instead of $40 million, it's maybe $32 million. If you ask me whether you should start today or start one year from now, my question would be, "Would you be kind enough to give me $7 million?" That's how much waiting that extra year would cost you. You should have that money going into your retirement sooner than that. You may think it's only a year, but if you think a little deeper, it's a $7 million dollar mistake. It's more than that.

Martin: Many people who are coming into the note space are coming in to build a better future for themselves. They want security, and they are trying to grow multiple streams of income. What you're saying is that if you're going to do it, do it with the best?

Chaim: If this is your life, and you want a better life, there is no better time than now. At the same time, start investing and understanding what is going on in your macro picture. Start being interested in people who are trying to take away money from you as well. It's not about what you make. That helps. It has a lot to do with how much you keep. When you see someone taking money away from you, you should know it's not just money they are taking away. It has a bigger future value than what's on the surface.

And if you have absolutely no choice but to do it, then OK. I guess you have to do it, but at least know your options. Try to give away as little as possible if you can. If you have a robbery, and you have the power to try and hide some things, would you still let them take everything? Do whatever you can to hold on to your money.

Martin: It's interesting hearing the philosophies and strategies you give us here; it's great to understand them and think of ways to set them up, but the challenge for most people is sustainability or the need for handholding over the course of time. What would you say to these people? We all could use a little ongoing support, at least until it's ingrained and becomes habitual.

Chaim: Of course. The best thing I can advise you is to surround yourself with people who best understand this. The first thing that you want to find out from any planner that you work with is how successful they are. Make sure you work with people who do this and who live this before you partner up with them. Make sure you are close to people who are accomplishing exactly what you want to accomplish. I guarantee you that if you get close to a lot of losers, you will become a loser yourself. A lot of people are very protective of their relationships.

I'm not saying you should abandon all of your relationships. But you should, at the very least, understand who it is that you are hanging out with

> because they have an effect on what you think and how much you can accomplish in life.
>
> The only other thing I'd like to add is that I'm honored to be a part of this book and have a relationship with you, Martin. Everyone who reads your stuff—and gets involved in your programs—is very fortunate.

Chaim's interview is crammed full of valuable nuggets of information. He provides a great sense of what you could be accomplishing. You will have to forgo procrastination and investigate new and exciting ways to make money work for you.

As you begin to do so, just keep in mind that there are several things that could destroy everything you've worked for. As Chaim pointed out, you have about forty million reasons to be bubbling with enthusiasm. There will, however, be some hurdles along the way.

In the last chapter, I will give you tips on avoiding the things that could kill your note business. This chapter is vital if you're full of passion to start investing or if you're a seasoned note investor who is starting to grow stale.

CHAPTER 10

◆ ◆ ◆

What Will Kill Your Business

Congratulations on making it here. Although this book outlines the tasks ahead, you're one step closer to creating a passive income stream and enjoying the kinds of things you've been dreaming about like financial freedom and freedom of time. Those were my goals when I entered the note space. I never intended to reign in that passion, quite the contrary. If your systems are good, and you're ready to give it a go, hold on to that. Before you dive in, I want to caution you about five issues that could kill your note business. If you've followed this book closely, these five issues shouldn't be a surprise:

A. Lack of identity and purpose
B. Unaddressed weaknesses
C. Lack of sourcing outreach
D. Failure to evolve
E. Lack of controls

Lack of Identity and Purpose

Many people say that a lack of cash flow kills a note business. As I've grown as a business owner and note investor, however, I've learned this isn't necessarily true.

Look no further than a lack of identity and purpose. This is a true business killer. I see many people enter into the note space with some easy or generic roadmap provided for them by some educational platform they've found. I see them getting lost and confused because generic roadmaps were designed for everyone and no one. I see people staying inside their comfort zone, and I also see people fizzling out over time.

I'll give you a great example. I'm no bodybuilder or fitness expert, but I have had good workout habits for most of my adult life. I was also active as a kid. In fact, just recently I went out and joined a CrossFit type of gym, but within the first couple of weeks, I sustained an injury. I look back on all of that and laugh now. I've worked out for years, and I had never had an injury up until that point. It came as a pretty big surprise.

I saw the CrossFit model, the sense of community, the intensity, and the focus on good work, and all those things appealed to me; however, it was not the roadmap for me. It ramped up too quickly, and I might have been better off sticking to basic aerobics or a StairMaster. It wasn't the right roadmap for me, and in no time, I sustained an injury.

Think about your note business. Know your own path. Stick to your mission and vision and take this seriously. I see a lot of people buying notes as a hobby. They may have read a few blog posts or attended a webinar, so they feel they can just buy a few notes and generate some passive income for themselves. You probably already know that's not going to work out well. Passive income is a bit of a misnomer. Sure, you can have passive income, but what are you doing to get to that point? At the beginning, it's not really that passive at all.

You need to have a robust business model for success. A lot of deal flow is upstream—at midlevel tiers. It's not free flowing on the retail level where you buy notes one by one. You will need an ongoing deal flow to offset fixed expenses; they don't just go away. You might get frustrated and end up selling your notes to someone else like myself. You don't want to do that, though I've seen that happen before.

Unaddressed Weaknesses

The second thing that really hurts people in the note space is the lack of focus on their weaknesses. Maybe they struggle with inner growth. Maybe it's sourcing tasks or poor outreach concerning strategic partnerships. Simply put, many people in today's world have difficulty with self-reflection. They don't have an accurate picture of their strengths and weaknesses. This is for a number of reasons, and it would probably require a whole book to investigate. I will say, however, that self-reflection on an ongoing basis is your best friend.

Take a good, hard look in the mirror. Before you start a business, before you invest time and capital—understand everything you need to do to have success. If you procrastinate for too long, your weaknesses will consume your business and may lead you to eventually give up as an investor.

Lack of Sourcing Outreach

Whether you do it yourself or hire someone, you need consistent sourcing outreach. It's not enough to comment on a few posts, watch some webinars, go to a conference or two, and hope you're going to land some good deal flow. You need to do much more than that to have a successful note business.

As we discussed earlier, it's still a very phone-call-oriented business, so be prepared to talk on the phone. That may be a weakness. Discover who you need to talk to, pick up the phone, give that person a call, and then record the results of that call. Think back to Alira's interview on project management. She puts all her information in her CRM.

Most outreach and sourcing depend on *your* level of output and due diligence. Platforms like Paperstac will ping you with deal flow, but relying on that solely will bottleneck your deal flow. It will not give you enough deal flow to sustain your business. Connections will.

Chaim's hypothetical example showed us that an investor would lose $7 million dollars by procrastinating in just one year. He used his calculator, plugged in the numbers, and put a mathematical stamp on one area of potential weakness. This is a big deal. Your life is on the line. Your freedom of time and finances are at stake.

Make outreach a habit. You might say, "Okay, I'm going to make these five calls on my lunch hour on Friday." Note that in your daily to-dos and, instead of broadly focusing on the hundred or so calls, plot out the five or so that you need to make on a specific day. Then you're going to do that again. Before you know it, you've made those hundred calls and then some.

You'll develop better habits once you start acting this way, but most importantly, just imagine the connections you'll make as a result of those calls. Think of the deal flow. Make outreach a daily habit and be specific about who you'll talk to!

Failure to Evolve

Failing to adapt, whether you're a seasoned investor or someone up and coming, will kill your note business. The market constantly changes. Right now, with so many buyers on the buyer's list, you can see folks scrambling. They are feeling pricing and inventory hikes. You hear excuses about how they can't manage the chaos of the marketplace. Instead, they should be thinking about how they can expand their outreach. They should be in creation mode as I am and think about how they can adjust their game to stay relevant.

Lack of Controls

Some people want to wing it. They may get some notes in the door, and they may ask the seller whether they can pull a credit report for them or provide them with a title report or some other research data because they don't have the systems or controls to pull it themselves. Some investors will gloss over the due diligence process altogether because they're only buying a few notes here and there anyway. But what happens when someone approaches them with a major offer?

"I have forty notes. It's an all-or-nothing deal, and I need to hear from you in seven days," they will say. If their systems are not set up to vet those notes, they're going to have problems trying to assess the value. Those investors won't be able to price them accordingly.

Think about how you're going to manage and service the notes you already have, especially as the borrowers reach out. You will need good systems in place to achieve a successful outcome. In my opinion, PODIO is definitely the way to go.

Putting It All Together

I hope all of these tips and strategies have helped give you a sense of the task ahead. It shows a lot that you've stuck with this process until now. Still, it's understandable if you feel unsure about how to get things going.

The best thing to do is to start with your living financial statement and then move to your MAP. Fill out your MAP timeline as much as you can and think objectively. Talk to your spouse or partner and decide whether note investing is right for you. If you feel that it is, consider rereading or referencing this book. If you're thinking about helping the borrower stay in their home with payments they can afford while building loan modifications that are paying you every month on twenty- and thirty-year terms, build your MAP so you focus on buying notes where your due diligence gives you confidence in the borrower's ability to pay. That was practically my mission statement when I started out and was what I did best.

As you get a better idea of what all of this stuff is about, plug more tasks into the plan, start following the steps, and build your systems in the control phase. The first two phases can be worked simultaneously. It's not linear. Commit yourself to strong habits. Start reporting weekly about what you did the week prior and what you're doing that week. That will keep you on track with the first two phases.

I wish I had all of this information when I was starting out. My wife and I began with a couple hundred thousand dollars to invest. We made some mistakes along the way. I didn't build strategic partners from the start.

I want better for you—to cut down that learning curve. If you happen to be thinking about some formal training, make sure to take it from someone who's in the niche you want to operate in. If you connect with me, I would be happy to refer you to the right coach based on your objectives. You can start with one mentor for now. You can find multiple ones later. You will be making some great connections. I ended up with one, Marty Granoff, but then I branched out and had several other mentors. Sometime down the road, you might cross-mentor someone and become accountability partners. Chaim Ekstein is that for me.

I want to wish you all the best and future success, whether in the note space or not. It won't always be easy, but if you work hard at note investing as though your life depends on it, you will prosper in this industry. You will find the financial freedom and freedom of time that you have been dreaming about.

If you're stuck in the corporate rut right now, and a quick exit strategy hasn't presented itself yet, just know that while note investing may not be a "quick" exit strategy, it most definitely is one if you play the game right.

Procrastination will kill your business, so make today the first day you declare yourself a successful note investor.

www.ingramcontent.com/pod-product-compliance
Lightning Source LLC
Chambersburg PA
CBHW050116210326
41519CB00015BA/3981